DANE RUDHYAR

The Galactic Dimension
of
Astrology

The Sun Is Also A
Star

AURORA PRESS

P.O.Box 573, Santa Fe, N.M. 87504

First published in 1982 by
Aurora Press Inc.
PO Box 573
Santa Fe, N.M. 87504 U.S.A.
Tel. 505 989-9804 Fax 505 982-8321
Email: Aurorep@aol.com
www.Aurorapress.com

Printed in the U.S.A.

Library of Congress Cataloging-in-Publication Data
The Sun Is Also A Star
BF1708.1.R837 1975 133.5 75-11852

The Galactic Dimension of Astrology
ISBN: 0-943358-13-2

Cover image credit: NASA

AURORA PRESS RUDHYAR TITLES

ASTROLOGICAL ASPECTS
A Process Oriented Approach
ISBN: 0-943358-00-0

**ASTROLOGICAL INSIGHTS INTO
THE SPIRITUAL LIFE**
ISBN: 0-943358-09-4

AN ASTROLOGICAL TRYPTICH
Gifts of the Spirit   The Illumined Road
The Way Through
ISBN:0-943358-10-8

The **ASTROLOGY OF PERSONALITY**
ISBN: 0-943358-25-6

The **GALACTIC DIMENSION OF ASTROL-
OGY**
The Sun Is Also A Star
ISBN: 0-943358-13-2

The **LUNATION CYCLE**
A Key To The Understanding of Personality
ISBN: 0-943358-26-4

PERSON CENTERED ASTROLOGY
ISBN: 0-943358-02-7

The **PLANETARIZATION OF CON-
SCIOUSNESS**
ISBN: 0-943358-16-7

Aurora Press exclusively distributes
The Astrology of Transformation
ISBN: 0-943358-49-3

AURORA PRESS

By DANE RUDHYAR

Art, Music, Philosophy
Claude Debussy et son oevre
Art As Release of Power
Beyond Individualism
Culture, Crisis and Creativity
Directives for New Life
Fire Out of the Stone
Occult Preparations For a New Age
Of Vibrancy and Peace
Paths to Fire
The Faith That Gives Meaning To Victory
The Magic of Tone and the Art of Music
*The Planetarization of Consciousness
Rania
Rebirth of Hindu Music
Return From No Return
The Rhythm of Human Fulfillment
The Rhythm of Wholeness
We Can Begin Again — Together
White Thunder

Astrology & Psychology
*Astrological Aspects, A Process Oriented
Approach
The Astrological Houses
*Astrological Insights Into the Spiritual Life
An Astrological Mandala
Astrological Signs
An Astrological Study of Psychological Complexes
Astrological Timing
*An Astrological Tryptich
Astrology and the Modern Psyche
The Astrology of America's Destiny
*The Astrology of Personality
*The Astrology of Transformation
From Humanistic to Transpersonal Astrology
*The Galactic Dimension of Astrology
*The Lunation Cycle
New Mansions for-New Men
*Person Centered Astrology
The Practice of Astrology

* Indicates a title published by Aurora Press

Contents

PART ONE

. I .

Introduction to the Galactic Level
of Consciousness

Some five centuries ago, Copernicus and Galileo envisioned a
solar system in which dark planets, compelled by gravitational
power, revolved subserviently around a magnificent central Sun,
the monarch of the sky. The entire system was thought to be
composed of material bodies moving in empty space—solid matter
in the case of the planets, matter in an incandescent state in the
case of the Sun. It was ruled by rigid mechanical laws. This picture superseded the older geocentric view of the universe according to which the Earth was the center and a hierarchy of celestial
spheres—lunar, solar, planetary, stellar, and divine—revolved
around it.

The change from the older to the newer world-picture has been
called the Copernican Revolution, though Galileo and Kepler
greatly contributed to its formulation and diffusion, and later on
Francis Bacon, Newton, and Descartes further developed its implications. The heliocentric system has been accepted everywhere.
Interestingly, the classical society which emerged in Europe during the late sixteenth and seventeenth centuries was modeled,

unconsciously no doubt, upon the pattern of the heliocentric
system: an autocratic king ruled with absolute power over a country which he theoretically owned and over a people subjected to
his personal will; and he was surrounded by ministers, courtiers,
and servants of various ranks reflecting his power.

A society and its culture are always based upon a set of assump-
tions which have a metaphysical and/or religious foundation and
which find their expression in great symbols and myths. In the
course of its development, an inquisitive and creative minority of
thinkers from the educated ruling classes—which in turn control
the feelings and religious beliefs of the masses—comes to question
the validity of some of the basic concepts they had until then
accepted as dogmas and paradigms. When this occurs, the revolution taking place in the minds of a small group of pioneers gradually induces and produces changes in the entire society. The way
of life of the people and the official mentality imposed upon the
educational system by a dominant intelligentsia are gradually
transformed. Various influences are always at work when such
revolutionary changes occur, some of which are produced by
altered material and economic conditions, by new inventions,
or by sudden changes in climate. But here we are concerned only
with the mental-spiritual transformation which takes place when
new concepts, new ways of interpreting old facts, or the discovery
of new facts, profoundly and irrevocably impel and, in a sense,
compel the leading minds of a culture to picture the universe and
life around them in a radically new way.

What Copernicus, Galileo, Kepler, and Newton achieved from
the sixteenth to the eighteenth centuries, Roentgen, Curie, Planck,
and especially Einstein and his successors accomplished less than
a century ago when, in a very real sense, they "dematerialized"
for us the universe in which we had implicitly believed for some
three centuries. A universe composed of solid globes of matter
separated from each other by vast distances and held together by
unchangeable laws of nature expressing an absolute causality
principle has become, after Einstein, a universe of fields of energy

(or force-fields) which only under certain conditions present to an observer the character of material solidity. The old "common sense" picture of the universe has almost entirely vanished in the rarefied air of group algebra, irrational numbers, and levels of infinity. More recently radio-telescopy has made us aware of incomprehensibly distant galaxies, quasars, black holes, and white holes. An expanding universe filled with all kinds of intangible vibrations and elusive particles, which might as well be antimatter as matter and operate in negative as well as positive time, is presented to our rather bewildered minds. Have we really accepted it? *Can* we accept it?

It took about two centuries for the Copernican Revolution to become officially assimilated, especially after Newton's concepts gave it more finality. As the number of scientists and the speed of sociocultural communication have immensely increased, the new picture of the universe—and an equally challenging change in the concepts long held concerning the nature and the innate potentialities of human beings—may become finalized and thoroughly authenticated before the close of this century; yet it is still being constantly altered and may still need to be redrawn on a radically new background. Perhaps it is still only partially valid. Should our present crisis of civilization lead to cataclysmic events, it may be that it will prove to have been only a transitional picture—destructive of old illusions, but not yet truly constructive because it has not yet found the essential key (or we might say, the *basic new symbols*) needed to bring significant order to an ever-increasing mass of as yet not truly correlated data which we consider to be facts.

But what are "facts"? The etymology of the word suggests to us that a fact is something "made" *(factum)*. A fact is what our means of perception allow us, as human beings, to be aware of. We know that if we photograph a landscape with plates sensitive to infrared or ultraviolet light waves we obtain a picture widely different from that which our eyes see. We do not see the immensely distant nebulae whose vibrations our radio-telescopes detect—or in a fog, objects which our radar outlines for us. Are these facts? And if they are, why should the nature spirits and the gods described by archaic men not be considered facts? Why should we not consider the visions of medieval mystics facts of *their* experience when we, as scientifically trained minds, believe nebulae billions of light-years away—or subatomic particles of which we at best see traces in sophisticated instruments—to be facts of *our* experience?

Archaic man built complex religious systems and cosmologies to interpret his facts in such a manner as would best give him a sense of universal order. So did the medieval Catholic saints— and so does our modern astronomer. Every culture builds the kind of world-picture that most effectively and convincingly produces for man's mind and for his deep feelings of being alive and creative the type of order to which the stage of human evolution which characterizes the culture can more meaningfully respond. That type of order is expressed in myths and symbols. Our present symbols are mathematical. Our myths are found in our Darwinian theory of evolution; in modern science's basic premise—unquestioned until most recently—that materiality and measurements are the only keys to an understanding of the world; and in our laboratory approach to psychology and medicine. Even the "self-evident" truths we have enthroned in national and international Bill of Rights (but which we actually do all we can to safely bypass or altogether ignore) constitute in the deepest sense of the word, a *myth*.

The implication of all this means simply that any society, any characteristic group of human beings, and in a restricted sense any individual person who is not merely an indistinct specimen of a particular racial, social, or economic type, perceives the universe as each one *needs to see it*. Man projects upon the outer world what he *potentially is*, yet does not yet know he is, in order to discover and actualize his innate potential of being. Man collectively "creates" the universe he needs, simply because he needs it in order to operate with optimum efficiency; and he does so whether he is an archaic shaman, a Sufi or Christian mystic, or a modern scientist in his laboratory or observatory.

When archaic man saw gods in the sky, it was because he needed gods to communicate with and enlist as helpers. If European classical man saw in the solar system a vast mechanism working according to quasi-ritualistic (i.e., unchanging) regulations—the laws of nature—it was because he needed an external and material sense of security to frame and bolster the development of his social individualism. When kings and emperors were overthrown, a sacrosanct Constitution took their place—or in religion, "The Book."

What man perceives in the universe, being a projection of his most characteristic need, is for this reason *a symbol of what man is.* It is a cosmified or deified image of himself; but it is more. As a symbol, it contains in a latent "occult" way the answer to basic human needs. It is an answer in impersonal terms—an answer formulated in a symbolic language, the deciphering of which is difficult. But the language of dreams and oracles also is and always has been hard to interpret.

What we are witnessing today is the gradual emergence of a picture of the universe which presents us with a special problem, for it demands the acceptance of *a new dimension of reality.* This "fourth dimension" can be defined by the elusive, yet revealing word: INTERPENETRATION. What is implied by it is that the universe and our total beings "interpenetrate." The era of isolated, irreducible, and quasi-absolute individualities, as well as of totally distinct and unrelated physical-material objects, is passing away. Everything not only connects with everything else; all there is interpenetrates everything. "Particularities" remain, in a space that is now seen as fullness rather than emptiness; but the basic reality is that space in which every particularity interpenetrates every other "in its neighborhood"—and neighborhood here may cover a vast field of interrelated activities.

Mankind as a whole, or even a sizeable minority of human beings representing an evolutionary vanguard, has as yet no *direct* experience of such a kind of universe. Organs of perception enabling us to apprehend in a completely convincing manner the type of *ordering, relatedness,* and *processes of transformation* evoked by the abstract mathematics of modern physics and astronomy are still lacking in "normal" human beings. The few sensitives or clairvoyants who can "see" or feel what most people cannot perceive are often not too reliable, partly because they operate against the pressure of the collective mentality of their culture; they lack a consistent frame of reference for their experiences. Mystical realizations, though generally pointing to a somewhat identical interpretation of a time-and-space-transcending Reality, have an absolutist and subjective character which makes them essentially uncommunicable. Communicability requires the possibility of formulating some principle of organization. The new experiences have to be referred to a new type of ordering, implying new modes of relationship between the elements of whatever "system" we are considering or participating in.

The new discoveries of physics and astronomy provide us with extremely puzzling data, which are in turn constantly being modified by new observations. The scientist is so conscious of the need to formulate new general theories that the very moment a new fact is perceived challenging some aspect of the until then accepted picture of the universe, he tries to make it the basis of a new model. Yet he usually lacks the imagination or the courage to free himself completely of the old paradigms of his culture. First of all, he finds it hard to give up the typical Western concept of the basic materiality of the world. Under the pretext that solutions must be simple and should not require the introduction of any unnecessary factor, our theory-makers fail to recognize their inbred cultural bias. It is as simple to say that the universe is a system of organization characterized by "life" as to state that it is all "matter" and that what we call life is an epiphenomenon or secondary product of the chemistry of material processes. We directly experience life, both in us and in all our environment. Everything around us is born and dies—even, for example, the mountains when seen in terms of the long process of evolution of the planet as a whole. We are now aware that even stars are born, mature, and die. Nevertheless, their life span is so enormous compared to ours or even to the life span of a society, able to transfer from generation to generation the knowledge it acquires, that a process which in a solar system takes many years may correspond to what in a human being lasts only a few seconds. Thus, H. P. Blavatsky in *The Secret Doctrine* states that the eleven-year, sunspot cycle corresponds to one single beat (systole and diastole) of the human heart.

The concept of hierarchy of "levels of organization" has recently been endorsed by prominent scientists. It has to be understood in terms of a "holistic" view of existence. This holistic approach, first presented by Jan Smuts and which I shall discuss in the following chapter, is now superseding or deeply modifying the "atomistic" world-view which, during the last four centuries, made separate and fundamentally isolated entities of everything—atoms, human beings, souls, societies, and events themselves. More and more, *the relationship* between these entities and their participation in a vaster whole—which in turn is a part of some still larger whole— is seen to be the stuff out of which "reality" is made. The concept of "field" is increasingly being used (and there is a very fine magazine published by Julius Stulman, founder of the World Institute Council in New York, entitled "Fields Within Fields Within Fields").

I have discussed this matter in other books; but what should be added here is that this holistic approach which is potentially transforming our image of the universe was developed and is spreading at this historical moment *because humanity needs it now.* The concepts which emerged from ancient Greece, and after a period of obscuration, became the foundations of the classical European universe which America inherited, cannot in their present form assist us in the now imperative transformation of consciousness, and at a practical level, of our increasingly obsolete socio-cultural attitudes and beliefs. We need to rethink most of what the pseudo-enlightenment of the eighteenth century brought us, if we are to save from our Western tradition whatever can be constructively used in the new global situation we are now facing. In order to do this effectively at all levels, and not merely as a makeshift operation, we need a new and all-inclusive frame of reference for our new experiences. We can discover it in the holistic and hierarchical universe which we are coming to know. This kind of universe is being revealed to us *because it is the mirror-image of what in us, though still at the stage of potentiality, is on its way to actualization.* Man always discovers outside of himself what he is about to become. Unfortunately, the inertia of past cultural tradition and of a knowledge frozen in rigid theories, forbid him for a long time to see and accept what represents the next step in his development.

We should not forget that the new mentality which took form during the Renaissance and became set during the second half of the European seventeenth century was given its basic form by astronomers who were studying the sky. European man then applied the concept of the universe as a machine to his behavior, and found in a central, all-power-dispensing Sun the symbolic justification of the divine right of kings—*le Roi Soleil.* Today, a new image of the universe should emerge from what modern science is only beginning to see at both ends of the scale of cosmic magnitudes—in the atom and in the galaxies. The nucleus of the atom mirrors to man the complex and ambiguous nature of his innermost self, while the vistas opening up as we probe the level of organization represented by spiral galaxies should indicate to us the possibility—and indeed the inevitability in a more or less close future—of a new type of organization of society, based on new modes of interpersonal and intergroup relationships. The problem nevertheless is, I repeat, how to interpret the recent revelations of astronomy and cosmology without allowing our minds to keep operating in terms of the old patterns of mechanism and materiality—patterns evoked by our inbred entity-making tendency and our egocentric and proud individualism.

It is here that, in its own special way, astrology offers us a symbolic picture of the process of expansion of consciousness and human behavior from the archaic tribal to the individualistic Euro-American stage—and beyond the latter, to that of a global civilization consciously and harmoniously integrated with all the infinitely varied yet interdependent activities taking place at many levels within the planetary organism of the Earth.

In the first part of my book *The Astrological Houses: The Spectrum of Individual Experience* (New York: Doubleday Anchor, 1972), I pointed out that astrology began as a strictly "locality-centered" system of interpretation of the facts revealed by the observation of the "dome of the sky"—a celestial hemisphere rather than a sphere, as there was no way of observing what occurred below the flat earth-field bounded by the horizon. Ancient tribes traveled very little from the soil from which they drew their subsistence; they were attached to the land as an ovum is attached to the lining of the mother's womb. Their cultures were moulded by the climate and the character of the local environment and all it contained. Men of the Vitalistic Ages felt fundamentally one with nature; they had not developed a sense of separation from all that to them appeared to be diverse manifestations of the One Life filling the whole of space. But they were led by the contrasting experiences of their tropical environment and of the sky to conceive this One Life as bipolar in its manifestation: earth and sky.

"Celestial nature" for them was the positive, creative aspect of Life expressing itself in a number of great spiritual hierarchies of divine Intelligences. Some of these operated directly through the Sun which, as it moved across the sky, focused the power of the twelve great zodiacal constellations. Other constellations gave more transcendent or spectacular (and usually highly disturbing) meanings to the space surrounding a few particularly bright stars. For these men of archaic time, celestial nature was the active fecundative polarity; earth nature the passive and reflective pole. The two were one in essence, and therefore men could communi-

cate with the celestial beings. These communications occurred in
a variety of ways—in visions; in great dreams, shared by at least
two tribesmen to prove their validity; in omens and oracles.
Astrology was, then, the language of the celestial gods—a mysterious language that had to be carefully interpreted, as dreams and
oracular pronouncements also have to be. It was a language used
by the gods to provide us with "information."

We can liken the information given to us by astrological charts
to that which the DNA molecules give to the cell. We interpret
this information in chemical terms because our mind has to interpret results in such a materialistic manner if we are to understand the life-processes within the cell. But evidently the astrological and the chemical languages are different, because they are
derived from different ways of approaching the universe. Yet to
say that all the life-processes we observe are the results of material
chemical operations implies the acceptance of undemonstrable
postulates just as does the attribution of these life-processes to
divine Intelligences. It is obviously difficult for the matter-oriented
mind to see the possibility of planets being the visible manifestations of gods conveying to human beings the type of messages and
organizational information which astrologers believe a person's
birth chart contains. The difficulty arises primarily because most
modern minds see everything separate from everything else—and
particularly cannot conceive of any "real" connection between
planetary motions far removed from the earth-surface and the
destiny and behavior or temperament of human beings, each of
whom is also believed to be a basically separate and autonomous
individual. For the archaic consciousness there was no separation
between the sky and the earth; they constituted the two polarities
of an existence which resulted from their unceasing and rhythmic
interaction—an interaction which the Chinese philosopher symbolized by the interplay of two cosmic forces, Yin and Yang.

It was only when human beings became increasingly individualized—especially through city living, which fostered ego-ambition
and thirst for power—that a new concept superseded that of the

unqualified interdependence between the two aspects of universal Life—sky and earth, gods and men. This was the concept of a basic structural analogy between the universe and individual man. The former was thought of as the macrocosm; the latter as the microcosm. They "corresponded" to one another, each developing parallel to the other; the macrocosm was seen as positive, and the microcosm receptive. Such a structural parallelism linking not too clearly two entirely different sets of events and characteristic behavior patterns has been given a modernized and restricted form by the psychologist Carl Jung under the obscure name of "synchronicity."

This Hermetic principle of correspondence, "as Above, so Below," probably developed in Hellenized Egypt, but it may have earlier roots. It formed the basis for a relatively new kind of astrological language, transmitted to Christian Europe mainly through the intermediary of Ptolemy in Alexandria, and also of some astrologers of the slowly disintegrating Roman Empire. When the Copernican Revolution occurred, leading to the classical heliocentric picture of the universe, a profound change took place in man's conscious outlook. What many people fail to realize is that this heliocentric transformation led to, and in a sense implied—though its founders probably did not realize this—not only a mechanistic, but a materialistic approach to *all forms of existence*. The important fact was not that the Earth became a globe revolving around the Sun instead of being the center of the universe, but rather that the *relationship* between every part of this classical universe had become *interpreted* in terms of the push and pull between material masses, represented as isolated entities in empty space. The universe had become atomicized, *because* Western mankind had reached a stage in human evolution requiring a powerful accentuation of whatsoever would justify and provide a logical as well as universal background for individualism—or we might say, for an "ultraindividualistic" approach to existence, whether at the personal or the social level.

The heliocentric theory introduced many complications into

the astrological picture. The shift from a "locality-centered" to a "globe-centered" study of the motions of celestial bodies led to a great deal of ambiguity concerning the nature of the zodiac and the astrological Houses. More important still, the new image of the universe as a machine essentially altered *the meaning* of the information astrology could provide. The mechanisticized sky, having become a vast cosmic clock, could only tell human beings the time—the time when *events* could be expected to occur —and, in terms of an imprecise Doctrine of Correspondence, *where* they would take place within the microcosm, the individual person. Classical astrology no longer dealt with "life"—and the Sun and the Moon which in earlier centuries had become the two sources of bipolar life-processes soon became, for the modern astrologer, mere members of the planetary group. The individual person was considered exterior to his birth chart—the individual soul being also exterior to earth-nature. A man was "wise" to the extent to which he "ruled his stars."

The break between individual man and the universe became more total in the nineteenth century. Man became drunk with pride in the progress for which he was solely responsible, and with the power placed in his hands by his analytical and inventive, but matter-bound intellect. It was only after the conjunction of Neptune and Pluto in 1891–92—five hundred years after a similar conjunction had marked the early beginning of Humanism and of the pre-Renaissance period—that the discovery of radioactivity; the theories of Planck and Einstein; the use of larger telescopes, then of radio telescopes, led to an almost totally different picture of the universe. The implications of such a picture have not yet been realized, except perhaps by a very few philosopher-scientists, just as the long-term effects of the Copernican Revolution were not understood until a century or two later.

Today, having created the instruments which made a new image of the universe possible, man has reached a stage at which he is in dire need of integrating the capacities which he has recently developed with the complementary faculties which he had to downgrade (and even reject) in order to concentrate on building his new powers of analysis, interpretation, and generalization. The direct results of the technology that enabled man to build instruments increasing a thousandfold his perceptive capability, is compelling him to challenge the exclusive validity of the intellectual and social approach that made the creation of such instruments possible. The technology is an outstanding success, but the next generation might die from its relentless application unless it reconsiders and thoroughly revises the premises on which our Western civilization based its classical image of the universe and of man's relationship to this universe. The recent scientific discoveries have not yet actually erased this image from the collective consciousness of most people, including the great majority of political and religious leaders and educators.

This does *not* mean that we should return to an archaic and naïvely "vitalistic" picture of the universe; and, in astrology, to a locality-centered type of interpretation of the sky filled with hierarchies of gods. It does mean nevertheless that the breach between man and the universe has to be *healed*—for it was truly a "dis-ease," intended as it may have been to rouse man to a feverish pitch and force him to overcome the inertia of the old tribal forms of social existence. *Communication must be reestablished between the universe and man.*

This can only happen when man feels himself a functional part of the universe and no longer a stranger in it; when man's experience of, first, life—then, consciousness, and intelligence—is understood to be not merely a chance accident in a meaningless universe in which material masses speed aimlessly at inconceivable speeds, but a basic constituent of the cosmos. In this cosmos matter, life, mind, and a supermental substance-energy which we vaguely call spirit, are to be considered and (eventually) directly experienced as different "levels of organization" of reality. This multilevel reality pervades the whole of space and is active throughout infinite duration. It operates cyclically, because it is dual or bipolar in nature, and what we call and experience as existence results from the unceasing interplay of two cosmic forces—an interplay that produces a rhythmic sequence of cosmic manifestations in limited space-time fields of activity—which periodically return to a metacosmic state of infinite potentiality.

The essential metaphysical features of such a world-picture are not new, but the picture as a whole has to be radically reformulated, so that it may better answer the needs of a humanity having developed a new type of mind and of interpersonal relationship.

A new formulation implies new symbols, or more accurately *a new level of symbolization;* and it assuredly is not easy to reach a higher because more inclusive level of conceptualization and symbolization. Nevertheless, it should be done and the elements already are available, being provided by the new discoveries in nuclear physics and galactic astronomy. The problem, I repeat, is how to use these new elements without reducing them to conceptual patterns belonging to the intellectualistic and mechanistic level of classical astronomy. It is a problem of interpretation— interpretation on the basis of a new dimension of consciousness, giving a new character to all the basic realities of human existence. The word I have already used, interpenetration, seems to be the best available to define this character.

From the point of view of an astrology free from the ghost of even the most sophisticated and "scientific" type of fortune-telling, this new four-dimensional approach to existence and human consciousness can best be symbolized by referring to the Galaxy—just as the classical European type of approach could significantly be referred to the Copernican and Newtonian picture of the solar system. Thus I am speaking of a "galactic dimension of astrology." It can also introduce us to a "galactic" concept of society and humanity, according to which our spiral Galaxy symbolizes the slowly emerging "Universal Community of Man."

.2.

When the Sun Is Seen as a Star

a) A Galactic Approach to the Solar System

According to a holistic approach to the nature of the universe and of humanity, what we call existence is a state of activity operating in terms of "wholes." A human being constitutes a whole. He or she is an organism, which means an organized field of interrelated and interdependent—thus functional—activities. We classify these activities according to whether they operate at a physical-biological, psychological, mental, and (for lack of better terms) supermental or soul level. Man, as a total person, is the whole that includes them all.

In man, this organized and organic field of existence has at least the potentiality of developing a unique kind of interrelationship between each of its contents; thus, an individualized character. This uniqueness expresses itself in the realization "I am this particular person." In man, therefore, the field of activity has acquired a center to which the most important portion of its activities are consciously referred. It at least seems the most important to the mind of the person experiencing these activities as his own. A mind is the form which consciousness, emerging from the field of activities of a particular person, takes—and maintains. This form is normally controlled by the ego, which refers to the particular manner in which the *centrality of the whole field* manifests at the level of what we call "waking consciousness."

A human being, as perceived by our "normal" senses at the present stage of human evolution, is first of all a body—that is, a biological system. The component parts of this system are cells, most of which operate in communities called "organs" (heart, liver, brain, glands of various types); others, in more loosely related circulatory subsystems or interstitial masses spread out wherever needed. Each cell is a well-defined whole with characteristic properties; it contains molecules which are also structured systems of activities organized for a specific type of work—and molecules contain atoms, which contain many elusive particles of various types. Thus, at the level of life in this Earth's biosphere we perceive a holarchic or hierarchical series of wholes, each one with a definite kind of function within the field of the "greater whole" of which they are a part. Each in turn constitutes a greater whole to its own component parts.

When a modern mind objectively considers such a series, it usually takes for granted that the series ends with the living body of animal and human beings. Yet all these living bodies operate within the biosphere of a planet which—we have at long last come to learn—is actually a remarkably well-organized system of constantly interrelated, interacting, and interdependent parts. These parts are the various "kingdoms" we clearly know and can observe (mineral, vegetable, animal, human). To these we should at least add telluric or planetary factors like atmospheric, stratospheric, and oceanic currents, and also magnetic forces or envelopes (the van Allen bands, for instance) which perhaps play a fundamental role in the harmonic operation of the entire planetary whole.

Besides these categories of activities, there may be other "kingdoms" or nodal centers of energy which our normal sense today cannot perceive. They may be considered "physical" at a different vibratory level, or superphysical. All followers of ancient religions, and many people even now living close to nature, and most present-day sensitives and clairvoyants bear witness to the existence of normally unperceived classes of entities coexisting with us in the Earth's biosphere, or in other spheres included in the total field of planetary activity which we call the Earth. They have been given many names: angels, devas, nature spirits of various types who may be the personifications of *guiding energy-fields* operating within the four visible kingdoms of life. Some of these "energy-fields" are perhaps directly related to solar radiations or other cosmic sources.

The belief in the existence of what seem to us normally invisible forms of life or intelligence was natural to men of archaic times. It has never entirely disappeared, whether in a naïve, a dogmatically religious, or a "paralogical" (i.e., occult) form; but it was exorcised by the high priests of our classical physics and cosmology in the name of a rationalism totally subservient to a materialistic empiricism. Whether this belief is or is not based on incontrovertible facts of objective experience is not essential at this stage of our presentation. What is important is that there seems to be no valid reason whatsoever for ending the hierarchical series of ever more inclusive (but always rigorously organized) fields of activities with the human body or, as Jan Smuts claimed in his epoch-making yet rarely mentioned book, *Holism and Evolution* (1926), with the individual person.[1] If we do end the series there, this means that we can conceive only of three levels of cosmic activity: matter, life, and personality (which includes mind even in its highest human form)—and this surely would be a remark-

[1] The words holism and holistic are now widely used by philosophers, scientists, and students of the arts, especially in contrast to atomism and atomistic. In my recent books *The Planetarization of Consciousness* and *We Can Begin Again—Together,* I coined the terms holarchy and holarchic to refer more definitely to the principle of hierarchy operating throughout a universe of wholes, every whole being part of a "greater whole" as well as the container and synthesis of a multiplicity of "lesser wholes." A holarchic universe is one featuring many levels of activity and consciousness.

able manifestation of human pride ("No one can be greater than I, man."), were it not for the belief in an all-encompassing God before Whom man is supposed to humble himself in utter devotion and self-surrender.

The image of God which Christendom has featured, a few exceptions notwithstanding, can be symbolically characterized as "heliocentric." The *theocentrism* of the theistic "great religions" —from which we have to except Buddhism in its original form— parallels the heliocentrism of the classical world-picture: an all-powerful, light-emanating Sun—the one and only source of light, heat, and radiation—surrounded by subservient dark planets; the Earth being the only sphere in which, through some fortuitous chemical good luck, living organisms and eventually men could develop.

Such a picture undoubtedly represents a definite and significant milestone in the evolution of human consciousness—as does the development of the ego in man, for the ego seems to be the inevitable form which the process of emergence of individuals out of the matrix of the tribal society had to take. A personal God, ruler of the universe and originator of changeless "laws of Nature" —the Sun, the great autocrat of his own system, the whole of which (the "heliocosm") he controls as his private possession—the ego of the individualized person, also ruler (in theory) of the personality and of the body that should be his obedient slave: at these three levels *the same* concept operates. This concept was needed in order that the process of individualization could work and man feel himself a "free and responsible" individual. Unfortunately, the ideal of individualism—which inspired the social-political concept of democracy—failed to operate at the level of a spiritual type of individual selfhood, a selfhood integrated within a universal community. Similarly, the heliocentric picture of the solar system, at least for a long time, did not stress the fact that *our Sun is also a star within a larger cosmic whole, the Galaxy.* And the worship of a personal God, an all-powerful Lord of Hosts may not be the most spiritual approach to the ideal of di-

vinity—as many mystics, especially Meister Eckart, have tried
to make clear.

The basic issue I am stressing here is that the classical heliocentric world-picture was a projection upon the dome of the
sky of the human need for an individual center within his personality—but a need which was inadequately formulated and which
made of the "I am" center of man's total person an autocratic,
proud, jealous, and warlike ego. This ego may inevitably be the
first step in the development of the "I am" center; but it is a
step that should be followed by another. A way to understand
objectively the difference between the ego and the spiritual center
of which it is at best only one aspect, is to realize that, as I have
said above, the Sun is not only the dominant power in his system
of planets, but also *one of billions of stars* in the Galaxy. In other
words, the Sun can be seen in two distinct roles; and likewise the
center of man's being can function, both as ego and as one of
billions of "I am" centers in the universal community of Man.

To come to a vivid, inescapable, and total realization that the
ego-Sun is essentially but one galactic star constitutes essentially
the first stage of the transformation of man, as in most cases he
is today, into "more-than-man"—and symbolically into a galactic
being, a "star." This transformation is necessary as the foundation
of a "Galactic Revolution."

When the Sun is seen as the star it fundamentally is, a galactic
frame of reference takes form in the consciousness of man, and
it brings to all the patterns and events of our traditional solar
system a potentially new meaning. The planetary facts *at first*
remain what they were. The orbits, the speed of revolution, and
the cyclic interrelationship between their positions in the sky seen
by human eyes do not change; but the interpretation of these
facts is altered. The long-used traditional names acquire a different meaning—and this unfortunately causes semantic problems.
The entire solar system is seen in a new light, the light of the
relationship it has to the Galaxy. This light brings into a sharp

relief the difference between the planets that revolve within Saturn's orbit—including Saturn itself—and the trans-Saturnian planets, Uranus, Neptune, and Pluto.

What I mean by *the relationship* which the solar system has to the Galaxy is the fact that from the "holarchic" point of view I am presenting, *two forces* are active within our solar system: the gravitational pull exerted by the Sun, and another force, the nature of which we may not as yet really understand, "galactic power." And this term, galactic power, should be understood to mean the power of the type of energies—and better still, of the *quality of existence*—pervading the whole of galactic space. The relative strengths of these two forces changes according to the region of the solar system one considers. In the region bounded by Saturn's orbit, the power of the solar autocrat is dominant; beyond Saturn, galactic power overcomes solar power. Yet throughout the whole system the two forces are active; they are active within man, because every cell of man's body exists in galactic space as well as in heliocosmic and biospheric space. The space of any "greater whole" includes the more differentiated spaces of all the "lesser wholes" which it contains and whose activities it organizes functionally with reference to its needs. In most instances the "lesser wholes" are unconscious of the needs of the "greater wholes," yet their overall life patterns (their "destinies") are subjected to those very needs.

If we truly understand this picture of the universe, we should see that central to it is the concept of a *hierarchy of spaces;* and space, during a period of cosmic manifestation, actually represents the manner in which all the organized systems of activities operating in any region of the universe are interrelated and interacting. Space is not an empty container into which material substances are poured; it is the interrelatedness of all activities. As these activities are operating at different levels of organization—or planes of existence—the *quality* of their interaction and interdependence varies with each level. There is a hierarchy of levels or scopes and rhythms of activity, and thus a hierarchy of qualities of existence. Existence at the biospheric level in the earth-field has a different quality or character than at the heliocosmic and galactic levels.

Thus, when I speak here of galactic space I am referring to the special character of the relationship between entities (i.e., organized fields of activity) which we call "galactic" because we perceive their activities as essentially different from and superior to those of entities that exist on dark planets radiating no light. These cosmic light-radiating entities we call "stars"; and our Sun is one of them—and by no means one of the largest and most brilliant or more centrally located.

Galactic space is space within which stars are related to one another. Heliocosmic space is space within which planets and other material entities are related to one another. Biospheric space is space within which living organisms enter into relationships with each other. These spaces differ in the character or quality of the relationships operating within them, yet the larger space contains the narrower; therefore man who normally acts within biospheric space is also pervaded with galactic space and affected by the relationship between the stars—though normally he is not aware of this. His consciousness does not operate at the galactic level; even less can he *physically act* at that level. However, consciousness is always ahead of concrete activity, the latter operating on a collective basis.

While physically limited to the tribal level of sociocultural activity within a local environment, human beings could nevertheless be conscious of what "life" in a general sense meant; and they projected that meaning upon the sky, which they saw filled with the One Life differentiating through creative celestial hierarchies. When, through travel, mankind became aware of the spherical nature of the Earth and of the biosphere as a whole, the consciousness of the more evolved minds began to picture the universe in heliocentric terms—and the classical picture of the universe arose, which then astrologers interpreted in individualistic and event-oriented terms for men who tried to act as solar autocrats—or at least as autonomous individuals. Today it is increasingly possible for men to overcome the gravitational pull of our Earth and to travel in heliocosmic space. Such a physical achievement becomes then the symbol of *the possibility* for any consciousness attuned to a quality of existence broader and more inclusive than the collective norm to reach the level of galactic existence.

Astronomy has provided us with visual material on which we can begin to build a picture of what takes place within galactic space. Such a picture at present is still uncertain and full of mysteries. Yet astrology can begin to interpret in symbolic terms *the relationships* between the stars moving within this galactic space.

Human beings are not stars, but what occurs in the realm of stars and in terms of a galactic quality of existence may be used as a symbol of a slowly developing type of human consciousness, whose more-than-individualistic—and therefore symbolically more-than-heliocentric—character can be referred to the quality of existence of the galactic dimension of space.

The essential factor in this transformation of man's consciousness is the transmutation of the "solar" I into the "galactic" We. In this We-consciousness the principle of interpenetration operates. This is the galactic dimension of existence. In it, the sense of the separateness of isolated (i-*sol*-ated!) entities (which are strictly and exclusively what they are) vanishes. Everything not only is related to everything else, but, I repeat, every entity—every mind, too—interpenetrates every other entity. As the consciousness of an individual person is able to operate in this spiritual dimension, it begins actively and transformatively to participate in the process of integration of humanity at the level at which the formation of a "pleroma" (or fullness) of Man is possible—the level of the spiritual mind or supermind. At that level unanimity in consciousness prevails, yet each participant in the pleroma—or as a true occultist would say in the "White Lodge"—retains the ability to operate.

This level of functional differentiation is symbolically that of the heliocosm—Sun and planets. The two levels—galactic and heliocosmic—are related not only by the fact that the heliocosmic Sun is also (and primarily) a galactic star, but by that other less obvious fact that the planets beyond Saturn (Uranus, Neptune, Pluto, and probably at least another planet I long ago named Proserpine) are *in* the solar system but not *of* it. Their allegiance is to the Galaxy. They are agents for the dissemination of the galactic quality of existence. I have spoken of them as "Ambassadors of the Galaxy"—but they are the kind of ambassadors at least part of whose function is to draw the consciousness of human beings toward the Galaxy. They are radically transformative, indeed subversive forces at work in the solar system.

A transformative kind of activity always has its place in any formal system of personal or collective human organization—and symbolically in the organization of any Sun-centered type of ordering. Neither is it absent from the biological level, where it manifests as the *capacity for mutation* in every living organism. It is present in the world of the biosphere, because at the core of the planet Earth, there must be a point at which the action of the Galaxy is felt. Because galactic space pervades all living organisms, the mysterious core of the Galaxy can reflect itself upon or within their innermost space which vibrates, at least potentially, to the quality of galactic space—the quality of interpenetration and of star radiance.

While biological mutations occur only in the cellular or molecular substance of the seed's nucleus, at the level of the human consciousness, the process of transformation of the heliocentric into the galactic mind seems to occur in a central region of the head. That region is directly linked with the "heart center" where the spiritual Sun of man—atman, Krishna, or Christ—can be symbolically located. The two centers are one, just as the Sun is also a star.

b) Planets of Organic Functioning

Once we realize that the Sun is a star, and as such participates as an atom or cell in the galactic whole and is firmly rooted in man's mind, it is easy to understand how the solar system naturally divides itself into two areas. The area bounded by Saturn's orbit and the one that extends outside of it and includes the trans-Saturnian planets, Uranus, Neptune, and Pluto—just as the life of an active participant in a national organism is divided between a private and a public part.

In the area bounded by Saturn's orbit and dominated by the power of the Sun, everything refers to the organization of a system ·of activity able to operate as a steady and relatively permanent organism. Three basic principles of operation are at work: 1) the principle of formal exclusion, which establishes the particular form of the living organism and the self-regulated character of its operations: "I am what I am, and nothing else"; 2) the capacity for self-maintenance and growth through expansion and metabolic assimilation; 3) the principle of self-reproduction, and biological self-multiplication—and at the human level, also of self-expression in creative symbolic activity within a sociocultural environment.

These three principles (or powers) are represented in astrology by what in the past I have called the "planets of organic living" (cf. *The Practice of Astrology,* 1970) or "planets of the conscious" (cf. *The Astrology of Personality,* 1936).[2] Of these planets, three revolve around the Sun outside of the Earth's orbit: Saturn, Jupiter, and Mars. Three of them, if we include the Sun as the fountainhead of the energy making life possible on our planet, operate within the Earth's orbit; the other two being Mercury and Venus.

[2] The student is referred also to two other books, *New Mansions for New Men* (1937) and *Triptych: The Illumined Road* (1968) for different approaches to an understanding of the planets and the solar system.

As the Sun is the center of the field of organic living, Saturn in the language of astrology represents the circumference—the boundaries of *any* life-field. Saturn's rings constitute a visually clear symbol of the circumscribing, but also focusing character of its activity. It is the principle of Form dividing the field of experience into *outside* and *inside* areas. Such an activity sets boundaries which at first and for a long time operate in terms of rigid and fearful exclusion. But exclusion is necessary as long as the organism's functions are not stabilized, and a sense of security is not established according to the organism's capacity to insulate itself from external materials which it should not absorb, because it cannot assimilate them. To assimilate anything is to make it "similar to" what is being functionally used in the inside area of the organic field of activity.

Between the Sun-center and the Saturn-circumference stretches the field of organic living. Jupiter, the largest planet of the heliocosm, represents the capacity to assimilate, and through assimilation, to expand. If the Jupiterian type of expansion is to be wholesome, it should operate within the Saturnian boundaries. Yet when the latter becomes overrigid or overexclusive because of fear or shock-producing experiences, the Jupiterian force tries to flow outward through gates in Saturn's walls by seducing or corrupting the keeper of the gates; or, if this is not possible or safe, it attempts to compensate for Saturn's rigidity by building in imagination some kind of heavenly field in which the Sun-force would spread across endless space without limitations or (at the level of mental activity) without rigorous definitions and logical exclusivity. Imagining such a kind of Jupiterian space-field extension is, however, very different from actually *transforming* Saturn's power. The mind may refuse to see or deny the existence of the fortified walls; but they still stand, and they remain an even stronger obstacle to the galactic transformation, because the Jupiterian will to expansion, seeking to ignore or deny all limitations, stresses more than ever the strictly solar aspect of the Sun. Because Jupiter only sees in the Sun the source of ever-greater abundance, the Jupiterian optimist or religious devotee actually becomes ever more unable *to see the Sun as a star.*

Jupiter finds in Mercury a helper, and often a conniving slave. The two constitute a coupling, but because they operate at a different level than the Sun-Saturn pairing, the meaning of their relationship is also very different. The Jupiterian power of assimilation and metabolism needs a system-regulating nervous system. Jupiter may be the successful manager, but he would be helpless without an efficient executive secretary, or a well-integrated bureaucracy, and today a battery of computers—all of which refer to Mercury's function in any complex field of organic living or socioeconomic organization. Yet if Jupiter tries to expand along lines of compensatory and unsound dream-activities— and these may refer to pseudomystical or exaggeratedly devotional experiences, inasmuch as Jupiter can be related to religious activity—Mercury may confuse as well as excite the Jupiterian type of consciousness by hiding the dream-quality of its compensation for Saturnian rigidity under the glamor of intellectual self-justification and magnificently empty words, or of specious arguments.

The coupling of Mars and Venus operates in terms of another type of organic function. Mars is the often but not necessarily aggressive desire to reproduce the particular and personal form of one's selfhood by stamping its outlines repeatedly upon some receptive or weakly self-defined entity in the neighborhood. It seeks to fill outer space with replica of what one feels one is. At the biological level, this desire is the urge to have an abundant progeny. We see it operating in the Biblical story of Abraham, who envisions the land filled with generations of people all descending from the seed-pattern of his physical and intellectual being. This is biological immortality. We find it a physical reality in the authentic uninterrupted line of direct male descendants from Confucius, spanning nearly eighty generations. It is also exemplified in the numerous descendants from Mohammed.

Such a biological self-projection is made possible by Venus, which traditionally "rules" over the sperm and ovum-producing glands, testicles, and ovaries. In its highest meaning, Venus refers to the creation of archetypes, which are "mind seeds." Occultists have referred to Venus as the source from which archetypal Man emerged. This archetype became *concretized* on our Earth which, as a planet, moves midway between Venus and Mars, and therefore symbolically represents the outcome of their conjugated activity. Mars delivers the goods which Venus engenders. As ruler over all outgoing activity, and therefore of the muscular system in all its subtle as well as gross manifestations, Mars depends upon Venus for directives; that is, it depends upon the *value-judgments* (good or bad, desirable or undesirable, to be loved or to run away from) with which Venus provides it.

In modern astrology, the Moon is often paired with Saturn, because the two represent respectively the mother image and the father image in a person's consciousness, but not necessarily the actual character of the physical mother and father. The Moon should be considered as the symbol of an organism's capacity to adjust to the ever-changing conditions of everyday living and to repair itself. If the Moon represents the mother, it is because when the human baby is born he or she is helpless, and it is the mother—or it may be a nurse—who sees to it that the baby lives in the best conditions possible. Later on, the grownup child should develop his or her own capacity for adjustment and adaption; and he does this through "feelings." These represent the higher and conscious aspects of the unconscious and compulsive instincts of a purely animal organism. The Moon may refer also to the spontaneous type of intelligence which is also a refinement of animal instinct and is almost exclusively geared to survival.

One more important factor is found in the heliocosmic field that extends between the solar center and the Saturnian circumference: the ring of the asteroids. Recently, the asteroids have been brought to the astrologers' attention and an ephemeris has been calculated for the larger of these,[3] but I already discussed the

[3] Cf. Eleanor Bach's book, *Ephemerides of the Asteroids Ceres, Pallas, Juno and Vesta* (New York: 1973).

asteroids' importance in *New Mansions for New Men* and, in a different manner, in an article published in *American Astrology* magazine in October 1936. To the astronomer, the asteroids are a very large number of relatively small chunks of matter revolving between the orbits of Mars and Jupiter at the place where, according to Bode's Law, a planet should be found. This law, popularized during the last part of the eighteenth century but actually discovered by David Titius in 1751, established a rather mysterious relationship between the distances of the planets from the Sun. It stimulated efforts to identify whatever was located in the region of the solar system where the expected planet should be found; and on January 1, 1901 the largest of the asteroids, Ceres, was sighted by Guiseppe Piazzi from an observatory in Sicily. Many others were discovered during the last century, and there may be many thousands of very small ones. The four larger ones are said to have diameters ranging from 118 to 478 miles.

The size of the asteroids is not the important factor in trying to discover their meaning in the total structure of the heliocosm. What is significant is the large number of them and the fact that they swarm between the orbits of Mars and Jupiter. It actually is the *place* which each planet occupies in the solar system—the region of heliocosmic *space* in which it revolves—that gives it its abstract or archetypal significance in the celestial language of astrology, especially when that place is also interpreted with reference to the Earth's orbit. Similarly, the functional meaning of any organ of the human body derives to a great extent from the position it occupies, at least in the archetypal form of Man.

From a holistic (or gestalt) point of view, it seems quite illogical to single a few asteroids out of the swarm they constitute just because they are a little bigger and more easily detected, even if they have been individualized by mythological Greek names. If one does this, comets whose appearances are seemingly periodical should be given an astrological meaning. The satellites of all planets should also be considered. What is important in the asteroids is that they constitute *a definite class* of celestial bodies;

thus we should see in their collectivity the manifestation of some basic factor or structural principle existing in at least a certain type of solar system, and thus constituting a significant "word" in the symbolic planetary language of astrology.

Such a word was revealed to man's consciousness during the nineteenth century, around the time when two other great words, Uranus and Neptune, were also coming into use because mankind needed them in order to better understand a newly developed aspect of the human personality. When referred to what was happening during the last century, this celestial word can be *translated* in our rational-cultural language as "fragmentation."

The idea that the asteroids were produced as the result of the explosion of a planet has apparently been challenged quite recently; yet it remains the most likely hypothesis. Even if these thousands of fragments did not result from a planetary explosion, they still can be referred to a fragmentary state of existence and consciousness—a state of *atomization and nonintegration.* If now we consider the series of planets from the Sun outward, the fact that this "asteroidal" condition of existence is seen to succeed the type of vital activity symbolized by Mars gives us a rather obvious clue to its meaning. Martian activity rushes ahead impulsively and emotionally. In it man's desire-nature and his muscles are tensed for aggressive action toward the attainment of whatever is wanted. But does aggression always reach its goal? Our environment is full of other aggressors who may resent and fight against our outward activity. Even if we do not have to fight in order to get what we want, we often scatter our energies in the pursuit of so many desired objects, too many interests, too many ex-centric yearnings; we become feverish with activity and haste, and our body and/or psyche break down.

As I see it, this is what the asteroids' belt as a whole symbolizes. However, the disintegrated or disintegrative condition which it portrays can be cured, and the cure is provided by Jupiter. Jupiter tells us that Martian individualistic activity in the pursuit of emotional satisfaction, or even of biological needs, can be transformed into group cooperation, through which success may be achieved, where relentless and ruthless personal aggressiveness would only lead to self-fragmentation and karmic bondage. The belt of asteroids may be a symbol of the karma of past activities that were inharmonious or spiritually disintegrative. Standing as it does at some kind of midpoint between the Sun and Saturn, it is a reminder of the material implications of heliocentric consciousness. Asteroids seem to be strictly material entities without atmosphere, magnetism, and internal fire—without life of any kind. May we not see in them the dark reflection—the shadow—of the Galaxy, whose billions of stars radiate light? Every material life organism casts a shadow. Every muscular Martian action generates toxins in the contracting cells. Has not the Industrial Revolution cast a deep shadow upon the collective consciousness of the Western people?

The fact that Uranus and Neptune were sighted within the same period that saw the discoveries of the asteroids should be considered significant, for the two discoveries refer to the realization, at least by a few free and open minds, of the positive and the negative possibilities inherent in the Industrial Revolution, and in all it brought to mankind. The planets Uranus and Neptune opened the way to a radical alteration of all the implications of human existence, both individually and in sociocultural and political groups—an alteration that can lead to a galactic type of consciousness and organization because whatever these two planets represent, they point the way ultimately at the "galactization" of mankind.

On the other hand, the asteroids symbolize the fragmentation and atomization of Western society and of its once-homogeneous religious and cultural tradition. When, in the twentieth century, Pluto was discovered and a great amount of increasingly smaller asteroids were identified, the centrifugal character and the explosiveness of individualistic claims and ambitions reached such a dangerous level that it had to be either brutally or subtly checked by some form of Plutonian totalitarianism—Fascism and

Communism, or in the "free" world, big business, directing men's minds and feelings through the use of relentless propaganda which deeply binds while producing an immobilizing illusion of freedom.

In the language of astrology, Uranus, Neptune, and Pluto as agents of the Galaxy may be very disturbing words, because wherever the Saturnian power inherent in all that has form and boundaries has become materialized into the fortified citadel of the human ego, these words refer to life-challenges and upheavals of many types. Nevertheless, the crises thus induced are cathartic means leading to an inherently constructive and potentially glorious end. Uranus, Neptune, and Pluto are agents of transformation; and at the human level, processes of transformation are integral parts of the total organism of personality. They constitute a fourth level of functional activity, whose purpose is to allow a fourth dimension of consciousness—the galactic dimension—to operate.

When this dimension operates in a sufficient number of human beings, a contagion of transformation spreads and in due time alters the collective foundation of culture and society. We are today witnessing the spread of a contagion of change with its feverish ups and downs and the attendant suffering. It should open the door to an inrush of galactic forces—a "descent" of spiritual, transforming power impregnating the global space of the Earth as well as mankind as a whole. A global civilization may then take form which symbolically would reflect the essential character of the Galaxy as a whole. By then, the Galaxy will have been understood for what it is *at its own level of activity,* and no longer only according to our present heliocentric perceptions and materialistic concepts. It will be seen and felt as a cosmic whole of radiant interpenetrating stars in perpetual transformation—a pleroma of dynamic centers of galactic consciousness that, whatever they may actually be at their own cosmic level, can be used as magnificent symbols inspiring men to become more than men.

c) *Planets of Transformation and Transcendence*

Any thorough process of transformation must deal directly with the energies which produced the forms requiring radical alteration. As we saw earlier, the three fundamental functions operative in living bodies (or even in steady sociocultural systems) are symbolized in the heliocosmic system by Saturn, Jupiter, and Mars: i.e., the principle which produced circumscribing but also focalizing, forms (Saturn)—the principle of assimilation and expansion within the limits defined by Saturn (Jupiter)—the power of outgoing activity serving the purpose of the organism and in man, the ego (Mars).

Saturn, Jupiter, and Mars, which move outside of the Earth's orbit, regulate the relations of the organism with other organisms and with the environment as a whole. The Sun, Mercury, and Venus, which are inside the Earth's orbit, refer to internal functions. The Sun is the fountainhead of the life force (*prana*) and determines its specific rhythm in the individual organism—thus providing the energy to whose expansion Saturn will set boundaries. Mercury symbolizes all mental processes, thanks to which the Jupiterian social sense can produce a language and a culture transferable from generation to generation. Venus generates archetypal values and gives moral judgments which guide Martian impetuosity and aggressiveness.

Each of these three pairs of function—and especially Saturn, Jupiter, and Mars—are the targets for a three-pronged galactic challenge represented by Uranus, Neptune, and Pluto. It is a challenge to transformation and transcendence, and more basically to a repolarization of *the psychic overtones of organic activity* and a reorientation of the consciousness and its central principle, the ego.

We spoke previously of the fact that every area in the solar system is also part of the total space of the Galaxy, and thus is pervaded by galactic energies. However, in any system rigidly lim-

ited by the Saturnian principle of formation on the basis of exclusivism and separateness, these galactic energies are of a nature
transcending the system's normal possibility of resonance. These
energies exist within the heliocosmic field in a mostly latent
state insofar as the everyday operations and the ego-consciousness
of human beings are concerned at our planet's present stage of
evolution. Everything within Saturn's orbit gravitates toward the
Sun; it is biologically oriented and conditioned by the compulsive
and instinctual forces of the biosphere and the even more material
spheres of our globe. The basic challenge offered by Uranus,
Neptune, and Pluto is that of realizing the existence of another
and opposite kind of gravitation—the gravitation exerted by the
galactic center. It is the challenge of accepting being reoriented
and repolarized. What the trans-Saturnian planets demand is
therefore a *change of loyalties*. This also implies a new perspective
on life and all its organic activities, a new sense of relationship
to all there is and to the bare fact of existence. Eventually, a new
sense of time and a new capacity for action in space—galactic
space instead of heliocosmic space—will take form in the consciousness.

Such a radical transformation may be interpreted by the modern
mind as a *raising of vibrations* which enable the organism to
resonate to galactic energies. It can also be seen as the removing
of a great variety of obstacles produced by the Saturnian ego-
consciousness and its allegiance to narrow concepts and emotionally binding loyalties. This occurs at the level of the individual
person and also in any tribal, provincial, or national type of
society, culture, and religion. Once these obstacles are removed
and the limitations transcended, man is able to respond to energies, feelings, and thoughts at a new level of great inclusion and
more spiritual valuation.

This process of transformation and repolarization does *not*
require that we move from the Earth to some other place. The
"new life" is not elsewhere; galactic space is not far away or above
us in some mythological, transcendent heaven. Galactic space per-

vades each of us. We live in it; but we do not truly understand this fact as long as Saturn and the ego make us blind and insensitive to it. *Saturn's facts obliterate galactic facts;* yet these two kinds of facts are essentially the same. But the man with a transformed consciousness sees them in a different light. Nothing is denied; everything is transfigured. Once the transformation is accomplished, the biological Sun is more radiant than ever, because we see it not only as our autocratic Sun but also as a galactic star. As long as our consciousness and identity is attached to a physical body, this Sun sustains us biologically, but when the transformation is achieved, this Sun ceases to blind us by its glory. It no longer prevents us from realizing the galactic fact that as an individual center of consciousness we are the physical expression of one star in the Galaxy. This star is our father-star, our spiritual identity within the vast company of galactic stars. To know this fact with indisputable and irreducible knowing gives to our living inner security and peace. It is true "salvation."

Today this process of transformation and transfiguration can be seen to operate at two levels. In its most essential aspect it operates within the individual person, a process which the occultist refers to as "the Path." It leads by gradual steps—the true great Initiations—to supermental consciousness and perhaps conscious rebirth in immortal selfhood. Today, however, the whole of humanity—and probably the planet Earth as a whole—are involved in a process of accelerated change of which some esotericists [4] speak as a planetary Initiation. This change can be related to the transition between two great ages, usually called the Piscean and the Aquarian ages—and perhaps between still larger cycles than the procession of the equinoxes. It is because of that change, and the development of intellectual powers which made the Industrial Revolution and modern technology possible, that the three trans-Saturnian planets have been discovered and the existence and structure of the Galaxy (and other spiral nebulae) has been ascer-

[4] Esoteric philosophy refers to theosophy, Rosicrucianism, and all other forms of serious Occultism.

tained. These planets provide us with new "words" in the celestial language of astrology, which can help us formulate the major historical phases of the planetary transformation.

The first phase occurred toward the close of the eighteenth century, when the divine right of kings and the value of the rigid forms of institutionalized religion were challenged. It has been called the century of enlightenment, because it brought to Western civilization new social, psychological, and intellectual ideals, and it opened the door to the Industrial Revolution that was to change humanity's way of life. The discovery of Neptune in 1846 symbolizes the character of all that was occurring in the Western world and, through colonialism all over the globe. If the Uranian eighteenth century shattered in revolutionary terms the established aristocratic and dogmatic patterns of Europe, releasing the potentiality of human freedom and true democracy— alas, only the potentiality!—the Neptunian nineteenth century in many ways, and as much as the present stage of human evolution allowed, dissolved the strongly entrenched loyalties of human beings to rigid class structures and provincialisms. It forced the larger industrialized nations to encompass the whole globe in order to satisfy their need for raw materials and foreign workers. The variety of racial-cultural "melting pots" thus produced should ideally have become alchemical retorts for the transformation of national and class consciousness and the emergence of humanitarian, nonexclusive, and international organizations, whether at the social-political or the religious level; but these largely failed in their attempts because of the power of entrenched Jupiterian privilege and the greed of ambitious men.

The discovery of Pluto in 1930 at the time of the great Depression affecting the whole Western world provided man with a symbol of what inevitably happens when nations, groups, and individuals keep relentlessly pursuing the way of ego-aggressiveness, lust for power, and sensationalism, refusing to surrender old privileges and obsolescent beliefs. The inner darkness explodes into outer violence and ruthlessness. To the "white" Terror, the "red" Terror answers with even greater cruelty. Deception and destruction are accepted as principles of conduct. Everything tends to be reduced to its barest essentials, but in spiritual darkness the essential becomes the absurd. The glamour of ideals vanishes, leaving what had failed to be true to the ideal totally denuded. Yet Pluto opens the way for eventual rebirth, wherever *chaos* accepts to be fecundated by a new revelation of *cosmos*, and a new vision of universalistic order takes form within the purged consciousness.

We may not as yet have reached a situation of sufficiently widespread chaos to make a *collective* acceptance of a new order possible on a large scale, but certain individuals can always separate themselves from the mass of humanity still wedded to the compulsions, the violence, and the repetitive patterns characterizing activities in the Earth's biosphere. Individuals can leave the highway of evolution where the process of transformation is slow and hesitant, and enter "the Path." It is always in some sense the Path of Discipleship—even if the guru is not active in physical embodiment—because it implies *both* the readiness and will of an individual to "ascend" toward a higher spiritual level of consciousness and existence, and the "descent" of a being operating at that transcendental level and, out of compassion, ready to help (and indeed to involve himself in) whoever makes a sincere and consistent effort to take the Path of accelerated spiritual unfoldment.

In the symbolism of astrology this Path leads from a planetary and heliocosmic to a galactic type of consciousness and activity. As the individual treads this dangerous and tortuous Path, he or she has to meet the challenges represented by the three planets, Uranus, Neptune, and Pluto. Whereas on the highway of life a man walks with all human beings more or less at his own stage of evolution, thus as part of a collective sociocultural tide which pushes him along through crests and troughs, on the Path of Initiation the individual walks alone, surrounded by invisible alien presences and encountering one test of sincerity, courage, endurance, and discrimination after another. He walks "in the footsteps" of many who before him have followed this path. He may meet the remains of some who have fallen by the wayside. In the darkness, he may have to feel the soil under him to make sure it is still "the way and the life" and not some byways leading only to glamour-loaded illusions or dreary intellectual deserts. Occasionally, he may have a glimpse of a star to whose radiance his deepest being resonates, or he may have the fugitive vision of a being watching over him and pointing to some yet distant summit ahead. Whatever happens, he has to "walk on"—the great injunction given by Zen Buddhism. He has to keep in motion, for mobility is health and holiness as well; and the motion seems constantly to accelerate, the walk more demanding. The demands increase in intensity and difficulty.

Why should anyone seek that Path? This could be done in two ways: positively, because he has seen a vision—however imprecise—of a superhuman goal to which his whole being responded, and of a state of being that fascinated his consciousness. He may have experienced the presence or the inner call of a radiant being who was both himself and far more than himself. Or he may have sought the entrance of the Path negatively, because of emotional rebellion, restlessness, divine discontent, or a total dissatisfaction with the highway filled with mass-men—or perhaps simply because, for no conscious reason, he had to. But, whatever may have started him on the Path, he has to meet repeatedly and at different levels the Uranian demand for *transformation,* the Neptunian call for *transmutation,* and the deep relentless Plutonian call for *transsubstantiation;* that is, a radical change in the structure of his mind—in the quality of his responses to every aspect of everyday life and interpersonal relationship and finally in the very substance of his inner, and eventually perhaps his outer being.

This threefold change in form, in feeling-response, and psychic-mental substance constitutes a redirection, repolarization, and reassessment of the person's loyalties. It has traditionally been symbolized by the metamorphosis of worm into butterfly. It implies a change of the level of existence—from the biological to the spiritual-mental, from dark planet to galactic star. A new frame of reference has to be built and thoroughly tested by crucial experiences. The old heliocosmic field ruled by the Sun and bounded by Saturn has to become transfigured by the realization that it *is* a small section of the vast galactic space. The ego-ruled individual must cease to consider himself the center of a universe structured by his desires and his fears, his ambitions and his frustrations. He must accept his role as a servant of a greater whole. Outwardly this greater whole is humanity, called by some occultists "the great Orphan." In a higher sense, it is the brotherhood of radiant "star-beings" who successfully have trodden the Path and now guide man's evolution.

The change is truly a radical metamorphosis and inevitably it involves deep crises. This means, in terms of astrological practice, that the presence of Uranus, Neptune, and Pluto in a natal chart refers to life-processes and events which can be regarded either as constructive challenges to transformation into the "new man," or as drastically upsetting to the "old man" in every one of us, and often as totally destructive of whatever did refer in social terms to the old order, or biologically to physical or psychological health. The positive and negative evaluations apply to what the planet represents in a chart according to its place in the zodiac and the house-circle; and either both possibilities or only one of the two may be experienced. As these three trans-Saturnian planets specifically challenge a double trinity of cis-Saturnian planets (Saturn, Jupiter, Mars—and Sun, Mercury, Venus), the problem of ascertaining whether they will actually refer to constructive or destructive events, or to both, can only be solved—and this only most tentatively—by also considering the positions of the planets being challenged.

URANUS challenges most specifically Saturn and the Sun— thus the circumference and the central source of the energy that operates within the heliocosmic field bounded by this circumference. Uranus refuses to accept the limitations to the radiating power of the Sun imposed by Saturn, whether it be at the biological level (bone structure) or at the psychological level of the ego and its exclusivism. Uranus does not affect the Sun as a star, but by overcoming or at least deeply upsetting Saturn's powers, it transforms the mode of operation of solar energy. Uranus acts in swift releases of energy which often have great destructive impact upon whatever stands in their way. It is, in a sense at least, an action resembling that of the lightning or, in other cases, of violent wind. It may strike unannounced Saturn's fortifications and thus the long-accumulated or carefully engineered defenses of the ego.

When Saturn's power and the old patterns guaranteeing the security of the ego and social privileges have broken down, Uranus can act as inspirer and as the capacity to adapt to the new rhythms of a galactically-oriented consciousness. Above all, its function is to keep the path to the galactic center open. It induces a state of total availability to whatever has to happen. Such a state of openness and availability stands in sharp contrast to the inertial, habit-dominated, and tradition-worshiping Saturnian condition.

NEPTUNE is the "universal solvent" of which alchemists have spoken. It dissolves all that Uranus has shattered. While Jupiter refers to the process of expansion inherent in all life organisms—and also in modern business corporations—and to the greed for the kind of power that never seems completely to satisfy personal ambition, Neptune represents the attitude of detachment from every quantitatively measurable object, or from social gains and prestige, demanded of every aspirant to a spiritual condition of existence. Nonpossessiveness and compassion characterize that planet, whose symbol is the sea. But in its negative aspect, Neptune represents glamour in all its forms, and intoxication with whatever *reflects,* and sometimes is a caricature of cosmic consciousness and of the unitive state which the great mystics have sought to describe in often confusing allegories. Mercury, representing the mind conditioned by biological or social-cultural drives, is adept at presenting us with reflections instead of realities. Neptune challenges our dependence upon mere intellectual abstractions and social-Jupiterian fashions in thought.

PLUTO's keynote—which few astrologers understand—is *purity*. Pure water is water containing no extraneous material; thus a pure combination of hydrogen and oxygen, H_2O. Pluto is the power that impels, and most often compels, any living organism and any individual human being to cast aside all that is not its own essential nature—its "truth of being," its dharma. It is therefore a strongly cathartic agent. It cleanses and purifies, and usually not in a gentle manner. If Pluto challenges Mars, it is because the latter represents the often intemperate desire to flow out to whatever Venus in us makes us feel attractive. "Martian" actions, however, most often result in reactions which bring to the emotionally outgoing organism or ego materials and thoughts that are foreign to its nature. Such a type of activity is haunted by the yearning for self-expression, an expression conditioned, if not entirely determined, by social patterns or mere fashions. Pluto forces upon our egocentric consciousness the realization of the futility and the danger of emotional and ambitious outgoings. It ruthlessly destroys all glamour. It deconditions us and leaves us bare and vulnerable, but—if all goes well—sober and purified.

As the disciple advances on the Path and becomes repolarized by galactic forces operating through the three trans-Saturnian planets, new faculties begin to appear within the broadened and heightened field of existence. What was only latent, as part of the vast potential inherent in human nature, becomes actualized.

URANUS can be related to a new faculty of vision—thus, to clairvoyance. The true clairvoyant is able to "visualize," usually in terms of symbols or of oracular messages, the character and meaning of any situation to which he directs his attention. The symbol he perceives has an inclusive quality. In principle, at least, it reveals the essence of *the whole* situation—not merely some of the superficial aspects of this situation or what the person, under the control of the Saturnian ego, thinks it is (or, even more, *wants* it to be).

NEPTUNE brings to the disciple on the Path at least the foreshadowing of what true compassion and holiness mean. It enlarges the consciousness so it is able to respond to all conditions of existence and to accept all there is simply for what it is. It transcends intellectual categories and class or color prejudices, because it operates on the basis of total inclusiveness and impersonal love—*agape* (Christ-love) or the compassion of the Bodhisattva who vows to help all sentient beings until they reach liberation from the Jupiter-Saturn complexes of separative and spiritually dark existence.

PLUTO, in the spiritually developed individual, symbolizes his "ultimate concern" for what underlies all existence, a supreme reality transcending all movements of existence that are the outcome of limited and limiting desires and local or transitory evaluations. It refers to the power generated by true occult concentration; thus to yoga and all related forms of self-discipline and ego-transcending meditation. It focuses all the energies of the living organism upon a center of immoveable consciousness. At this center, the power of the galactic center—the divine within, yet beyond us—can be experienced. Upon this point, the star—which every individual human being potentially is—can focus its light. And the star's galactic rhythm may be felt by the whole organism, now able to resonate to it, in the silence of all neutralized motions and emotions.

When Uranus, Neptune, and Pluto have done their work, the boundaries of the heliocosm—the protective but isolating outer layers of the disciple's aura—have become translucent. Galactic light can pour through them without any resistance. *The chemical energies of "life" have been transmuted into the nuclear forces of "spirit."* Man, though still "in" the world, is no longer "of" the world.

When a sufficient number of individuals have reached that state, a transformation of the physical aspect of our planet will inevitably, yet gradually, take place. The galactic community of Man, of which some eighteenth-century visionaries dreamed, can become a fact.

·3·

The Uranus-Neptune Polarity

There are many ways in which a detailed study of the trans-Saturnian planets can be undertaken, as they symbolize complex types of activities. These activities inevitably have a complex character because they have to meet the extremely varied forms of resistance to any radical process of transformation which a human being develops. Both Saturn and Jupiter, at the social, ethical, and religious level, and Mars and Venus at the level of most personal responses to the challenges of everyday life, operate on the principle of inertia; that is, of resistance to change. Established patterns of behavior (habits) and of feeling and thinking (such as psychological complexes) rarely allow for smooth transformation whenever the validity of fundamental beliefs, paradigms, or taken-for-granted scientific postulates is seriously questioned. To whatever is enthroned as "the good," the "better" appears as a potential if not actual enemy, and the most difficult decisions are those in which a man must choose between an unfamiliar better and the traditional good. The essential characteristic of man is that, consciously and deliberately, he may always become greater. This is human majesty (from the Latin *major*, meaning "greater"), and this capacity for progressive self-transformation—for giving up the *merely great* to the greater—is represented by the Uranus, Neptune, and Pluto planets. In this and the following chapter some of the most significant manifestations of the transformative power represented by these planets will be discussed. Others could be added, but these should be sufficient to provide a basis for a study in depth of experiences which, though they may upset the balance and normal operation of body and mind, should always be interpreted as processes of personal growth, expansion of consciousness, and spiritual development—even if these lead to what seem, for the mind unable to reach beyond Saturnian normality and Jupiterian concepts of ease and success, to be failure, illness, or death. Apparently negative results, when reinterpreted in terms of galactic consciousness and of the relationship between events on our dark planet and the evolution of the star representing an individual's essential being, will be understood to be cathartic, karma-neutralizing, and thus liberating factors in the total process of soul-evolution leading to eventual perfection and conscious participation in galactic activities.

As one studies the operations of the trans-Saturnian planets, one should first realize that Uranus and Neptune stand as polar opposites. It is also significant that the two centuries which witnessed their discovery have also opposite, yet in a sense complementary, historical meanings—the eighteenth century being characterized by its brilliant but abstract intellectuality, the nineteenth by its romantic emotionalism, and the chaotic upheavals resulting from the Industrial Revolution and the release of new and transforming energies, psychic as well as material. Briefly stated, Uranus is the prophet of individualism and of the social togetherness of self-determined "free" man. Neptune symbolizes the often compulsive and unrecognized pressure of collective factors and mass-movements upon the individual, a pressure which tends to dissolve the integrity of the personality into the oceanic currents of emotions or imprecise, universalistic utopian feelings aroused by fascinating visions or charismatic personalities.

Individual and Collective constitute two poles between which all existential wholes oscillate, each alternatively waxing and waning in strength.[1] Within the heliocosmic field of activity bounded by Saturn, the individual factor is stressed by Venus and Mars; the collective by Jupiter and Saturn, the social planets. In its most essential aspect, Venus represents the type of activity that builds the archetypal forms defining the individuality of particular systems—biological species or individualized human personalities.[2] At the level of the transformative process leading from the sense of being "I" to the steady realizing of the spiritual "We"-consciousness, Uranus releases the spiritual light that for a moment may bring illumination to the Saturn-bounded mind; and when that transcendental light becomes more steady, the liberated consciousness begins to perceive the outlines of vast, nonexclusive patterns of organization, which are Neptunian in character. As the power of Neptune increases, the dominance of the spiritual brotherhood over the individual participant also becomes stronger. Unanimity (literally, "one-soulhood") supersedes individuality (or majority rule) in all basic decisions of the group. As a result of such decisions, cosmic patterns (rather than laws) are established or put in operation, which refer to the galactic aspect of Pluto.

Very often, when the trans-Saturnian planets begin to operate within the field of consciousness of man—whether of an individual person or a national-cultural organism—their operation at first takes on a destructive character. To speak in Jungian terms, they act in their "shadow" aspect. Uranus creates revolu-

[1] Cf. in Rudhyar's *Astrology of Personality* (New York: Doubleday Anchor, 1971), the Chapter "Individual, Collective and Creative"; also, with reference to the cycle of the zodiac and the seasons, *The Pulse of Life* (1942).

[2] We are told by many true occultists that the spiritual seed of conscious and independent human selfhood was, as it were, sown upon the earth some eleven million years ago by great beings from Venus, *the Kumaras*—such a process corresponding in Greek mythology to the daring act of Prometheus, giver of the divine fire of self-consciousness to mankind.

tionary upheavals in the psyche-mind, as "the contents of the unconscious" rush into the consciousness, overwhelming the protective barriers of common sense and rationality built by the ego, according to collective traditions. What, at the spiritual-galactic level, is the individually and consciously accepted unanimity of the Universal Brotherhood (the White Lodge) becomes the irrational, compulsive, and coercive power of a crowd, easily whipped into an emotional singleness of violent activity by a charismatic leader. At this shadow level, Uranus is the revolutionist, Neptune the mass-emotion he arouses, and Pluto the ruthlessness and cruelty of totalitarian or gang rule.

In the life of an individual struck by Uranian releases of galactic power, Neptune refers to the irruption of until-then unconscious, or repressed, ideas and impulses invading his consciousness, and in some instances causing an ecstatic state. The individual is thrown out of his normal cultural-rational state of mind by the Uranus impact, and he finds himself in a totally unfamiliar, perhaps frightening, perhaps exhilarating, psychic condition. In this state, his sense of "being I and only I" tends to dissolve into what he may interpret as cosmic consciousness. He seems to have reached the "unitive state" of which great mystics have spoken allegorically; or at least a high peak experience, such as the psychologist Maslow described.

The experience unfortunately does not last; and the individual usually finds himself once more sitting, perhaps bewildered and doubting of his sanity, within the familiar Saturnian ego-fortress. It is what happens *then*—how he interprets, or realizes in depth, the meaning of the transcendent experience—which gives it a constructive or temporarily destructive character. If the individual consciousness can assimilate the contents of the experience and, consciously or not, does not fear its reappearance, the experience should be eminently constructive. It can only be so if what it reveals can be referred to a philosophical world-view or a religious teaching enabling the individual to accept the possibility that this revelatory experience is part of a legitimate process of spiritual unfoldment.

If the experience is understood to fit in a scheme which, even if unusual in terms of the lives of ordinary people, can be endowed with basic meaning and perhaps with great value, then it can be interpreted as—and therefore it becomes—a step on the Path of self-transformation. For this reason, as modern man is caught in a whirlpool of radically transformative forces, a frame of reference within which these forces can be given a constructive meaning is very much needed. It is in answer to such a need that this book has been written. Astrologers assign the constantly increasing upheavals affecting individuals, groups, and nations to Uranus, Neptune, and Pluto, but most of them are unable to interpret these planets in terms of a realistic galactic frame of reference, because they do not understand the relationship between these three planets and the Galaxy. They believe them to be mere members of the solar system, as all the other planets are; they do not understand how the level of interpretation changes when the trans-Saturnian planets are considered "agents" of the Galaxy, and the Sun only one star among billions of other galactic stars.

Uranus is essentially the Awakener. Some three thousand years ago in ancient India, a group of Forest philosophers-mystics sounded a powerful call: "Awaken! Arise! and seek the Teacher." Their subjective spiritual experiences had made them realize the identity of the individual self with the universal Self, of atman with Brahman; and they sought to share this realization with those who could be moved out of their traditional ruts by the belief that such a sharing was possible. Today, because astronomy enables us to see that our heliocosm (of which the Earth is a dark planetary component) is but a relatively small organic whole within the vastly greater cosmic whole of our Galaxy, we have in this fact a symbolic way to give a constructive meaning to traumatic experiences so frequent in the lives of modern individuals and nations. We can integrate these experiences within a rationally explainable and ordered process—a process which began with the many forms of Uranian awakening that aroused mankind to a new realization of the immense powers—galactic powers—latent within him.

What ancient Hindu seers envisioned and yogis sought to achieve by complex techniques of biopsychical control can now be given a new and cosmic formulation. An awakening to galactic consciousness is upon us. We can accept it and *all* its consequences, light or dark, according to an expanding astrology, provided we interpret what we have been awakened to see in terms of a frame of reference based on the concept of man's spiritual evolution from dark planet to radiant galactic star.

To be awakened by Uranus is not enough; we have to learn to use our true Neptunian perceptions. We have to go beyond the merely cogitative, analytical, and discursive mind, to the "seeing" mind. I have spoken of it as the *clairthinking* mind, the mind of the seer who can *directly experience* ideas, symbols, and archetypes that interpenetrate and whose scope is universal, or at the very least galactic. Faced by such galactic realities the consciousness can expand and realize perhaps not the identity of the individual self and the universal Self—for this may not necessarily be the ultimate fact of existence—but the *interpenetration* of all selves and all forms within an all-inclusive cosmic whole. This is the great Neptunian experience. Man must *awaken* spiritually as an individual; he has to be born "alone" into any new realm of existence and activity—even if surrounded by, to him, invisible presences assisting his emergence. But consciousness (literally, "knowing together"; *con-scio*) depends on interrelatedness. Conscious thinking requires some kind of language of symbols or images; and all languages are produced by communication between participants in group activity—even if the group is represented only by a pair of communicants.

Communication and all modes of information—from animal cries and gestures to the most complex forms of astrology and mathematics—imply at root group activity; and at the most metaphysical and universalistic level, the emergence of a new universe out of the undifferentiated and infinite "Ocean of potentiality" results from the operating of the cyclically developing relationship between the pair, Spirit and Matter, or in Chinese philosophy between Yang and Yin. At the level of the process of transformation which this book is studying, this relationship between the two ultimate principles of existence can be symbolized by the cyclic interactions of Uranus and Neptune. At the sociocultural level it is the relationship between inspired individuals (avatars, geniuses, heroes [3] and the social community out of which they have emerged. The character of this relationship becomes externalized by Pluto. *The character of Pluto's activity is determined by the nature of the Uranus-Neptune relationship.*

Pluto always tends to finalize and make irrevocable what Uranus began. It does this especially when, for some twenty years, Pluto comes closer to the Sun than Neptune—a period of "spiritual" fecundation of the collective Neptunian mentality; and we are now about to enter such a period. But "spiritual" here may mean destruction as well as construction; just as in Hindu mythology Siva is both transformer and destroyer, a symbol of the universal process of death-rebirth. If the Neptunian collective mentality of a society, class, or group has readily opened itself to the new vision provided by its creative personages (creative at one level or another), Pluto reveals *a new center of integration* vibrating with galactic consciousness and power. If Neptune has brought very little or nothing except fallacies, glamour, confusion, and degeneration, Pluto reduces everything to chaos, often after a more or less brief period of compulsive ganglike subservience to a darkly powerful and totalitarian leader.

Between these two extremes of spiritualization and decay, there are varied possibilities of Plutonian activity—as, for instance, the highly Plutonian Nixon administration and its debacle after Watergate. In its cathartic or disintegrative aspect, Pluto operates on the basis of the fear produced by Neptunian developments—

[3] Cf. *Rudhyar's Occult Preparations for a New Age* (Quest Books, 1975), Chap. 8, "Two Polarities of the Spiritual Life."

for instance, the social fear of Communism or the personal fear of illness or failure. This fear, as should be evident by now, is very often aroused by those forces that would use it for their own advantage.

Uranus: The Constructive Value of Inconsistency

The operation of the type of occurrences and of inner developments which can be characterized as Uranian can be further elucidated if we relate them to what is usually spoken of as "inconsistency." A series of events reveals a "consistent" trend (from the Latin *con-sisto,* meaning "standing together") when all these occurrences fit nicely together and none of them sharply points in a new direction. Likewise such a series is continuous when there is in it no break, no hiatus.

It has been said, however, that consistency is the hobgoblin of little minds; and this saying has often been used by minds thrown out of gears by emotional impulses to justify their changes of attitude or policy. As is the case with many words, inconsistency may have a positive as well as a rather negative or pejorative meaning. It should be evident that there are numerous instances in which a sudden (Uranian) break with a long-standing and taken-for-granted policy has a most constructive value, provided this break—this "solution of continuity"—is necessary. The reason why it is necessary does not need to be consciously perceived by the inconsistent actor or thinker; he may operate intuitively and/or spontaneously, and only later realize what justified the act or the thought—or even, in some cases, the feeling—appearing to be inconsistent with his previous behavior, thought-processes, or feelings. Justification here means that what seemed inconsistent seen from a narrow (Saturnian-Jupiterian) field of consciousness was actually relevant and logical when understood in terms of a larger frame of reference.

Every truly creative act implies some degree of discontinuity.

It may mean, colloquially speaking, getting out of a rut. It may be called a mutation. Yet to the conservative, bound to an obsolescent tradition and refusing to recognize the necessity for basic changes, the creative, transforming act may seem inconsistent. It has been said that a conservative is a person who does not believe that anything ever happened for the first time. He fails to accept the fact that, within any particular cycle of growth, there must always be first times. There are always dawns which do not seem consistent with what had been known the evening before, because during the night some experience—most likely, unremembered by the waking consciousness—introduced an as-yet-unexperienced sense of contact with a greater reality or the realization of a wider, more inclusive purpose for living and acting.

What happens during the "night of consciousness" may seem during the day an incomprehensible mystery to a mind filled with social activities structured by collective traditional patterns; yet if the remembered inner occurrence can be seen in the light of the possibility of taking a step ahead in one's evolution, a new sense of order and meaning will gradually and inevitably emerge. A new orientation—i.e., a turning toward a new orient, a new dawn-point—will be experienced and the resistance of the past will be overcome. The Uranian inconsistency will be seen to be the prelude to, or the dawn of a new and higher consistency— a galactic consistency.

Such a discontinuous and perhaps sudden change of level may demand of the individual that he takes a steep step at the threshold of the new field of activity. Thus he may, because of fear, impatience, or spiritual ambition, miscalculate the height of the step and either fall unconscious across the threshold or even plunge into the abyss his unpreparedness opened to him.

Inconsistency can also be symbolized by a waterfall—a deep "solution of continuity" in the river's normal flow toward the sea. Such a discontinuous or inconsistent step nevertheless can be used by the engineer to generate electric power, bringing light to a city and enabling men to work consciously during what otherwise would have been nights of consciousness—thus perhaps making possible a step ahead in the development of man's collective mentality. Here we have a symbol of the transference of man's center of consciousness from the purely "natural" to the "mental-creative" levels of activity and consciousness—a symbol also of the descent of galactic power seeking to reach through Uranus the level of Earthbound consciousness in man. Uranus *focalizes* the power of the Galaxy, somewhat as a lens focuses the diffused energy of solar rays and generates an area of relatively intense heat in which combustible materials may be inflamed. The work of great geniuses, of men of heroic will, and of great avataric manifestations of the Divine will and purpose, essentially consists in becoming *focusing agencies* through which what constitutes at any time "the next step" for humanity becomes visible and fascinating.

This principle of focusing energy and of release of creative Words *(logoi)* is at the root of any mode of existence, whether at the macrocosmic or the microcosmic level. Modern physics has revealed to us that releases of energy do not occur continuously, but instead in small "packages" or *quanta*. Existence is cyclic and discontinuous, even though man is intent upon stressing its seeming continuity, because he fears the unknown and whatever challenges what his security-haunted ego forces his consciousness to accept as normality.

In Asia where the process of inwardly turned meditation is widely accepted as a means to self-transformation and the exorcising of the dark ego-will, much stress has been placed upon the fleeting moments that may occur between continuous and causally consistent trends of thought. These are the symbolical waterfalls in the flow of consciousness, the unexpected pauses in the melody of the thinking mind. It is *through* these very brief moments, some of which may seem "timeless," that the consciousness may free itself from bondage to the world of cause and effect and repetitive living. It is at these "holes" in the bread of life—holes produced by the "leaven" of spiritual contagion from teacher to pupil, even at times from lover to lover, or friend to friend—that the transformative energies of the Galaxy operate. They operate because only that which has become empty of lower nature's contents can resonate to the voice of the Galaxy. This voice sounds forth continuously through every cell of our being; because we indeed "live, move, and have our being" in galactic space. But we cannot hear, as long as our attention is totally turned toward the Sun, our lord and master. To be able to levitate toward our star, we have for an instant to neutralize solar gravitation. We need not go anywhere or generate any power. All the power we need is here. We have only to break our bondage to the lesser forms of gravitation—terrestrial and solar. This means, first of all, to stop believing in the inevitability of our subservience to these forms, to become inwardly still, and *to let* the vibrations of galactic space impress themselves upon our consciousness in their purity, their simplicity, their transcendence.

To let it happen: this is the key. We must let Uranus' invisible light become radiance within our silence. We must accept the discontinuity, the inconsistency, the paradoxes of spiritual existence. We must consent to be "waterfalls," even though it meant being deeply bruised by the rocks and the shock of plumbing into the depth, because what in us falls may be redeemed into light and illumine the minds of all men. Uranus demands of us the sacrifice of the waterfall, and we must let it happen. This is the supreme inconsistency: that the noise and passion of the waterfall is, to galactic ears, the silence that the Divine at last can fecundate. At the core of the hurricane there is silence and stillness—and so it is at the heart of all crises truly accepted and welcome. Welcome to Uranus, the heart of all crises of transformation!

Neptune: The Deconditioner Dreamer of Great Dreams

Most people do not sufficiently realize how we are conditioned since birth by the scenes surrounding us, the feeling in the words we hear, the examples we instinctively imitate, the language necessary for our potential intelligence to develop, and all the explicit or implicit, consciously or unconsciously accepted traditions of our society. In order to free ourselves from this protean impact of our physical, emotional, psychic, and intellectual environment, we have to experience an often long, tedious, or cathartic process of *deconditioning*. Neptune, which in one of its aspects represents the power of the collectivity over the individual, also symbolizes, in its higher aspect, the process of deconditioning. This may seem paradoxical but, as already stated, all spiritual processes involve paradoxes and the transmutation of a lower into a higher order. Such a transmutation may result from a repudiation of—or, negatively, an escape from—what has conditioned us; but, as the Tantric way of life in part of India and Tibet taught, we may also consent to experience some of the conditioning factors in a nonegocentric and ritualized (i.e., impersonalized) manner, realizing that we only are totally free of anything when we are able to experience it without any personal attachment and motivation; for thus not only are we no longer its slave, but we also fully and existentially "know" its meaning and strength, having matched this strength with our own and having overcome its compulsions.

This Tantric process undoubtedly is dangerous, and it has led to wholesale failures. In order to succeed, it requires a powerful capacity to visualize the ideal, superpersonal, and cosmic reality of what is behind the conditioning. It demands an outstanding and rarely found ability to see the whole in the part, the universal in the evolving particular, and to identify one's inner self and consciousness with the transcendent future even at the very moment one experiences the legacy of the past—accepting this past as a necessary prelude to the future and thus not shrinking from the experience because inwardly free from its binding power.

In order to identify one's consciousness with the future one must make a singularly powerful image of this future; or rather this image must be powerfully and ineradicably stamped upon the conscious mind by the power of the "greater whole" within which we live, move, and have our being. The stamping process often takes the form of a "great dream"—a dream which to the awakened consciousness has the character of a transcendent reality, a "divine" revelation. In this sense, Neptune refers to the great dreams of men who have not only envisioned, but have felt inwardly compelled to try to establish within, or at the fringe of our society what ordinary people often dismiss as "utopias." Yet such utopias, even though they may not withstand the pressures of the present-day society and the scorn of its sheeplike votaries or ambitious predators, are heralds of a more or less distant future. The great dream of Neptunian visionaries become the reality of freer and more glorious tomorrows. They serve a potent purpose because mankind can never become what some men at least have not envisioned. Nothing can ever take place in concrete, actual reality that at least two or three men have not previously imagined and formulated in at least tentative outlines.

The Neptunian paradox is that freedom most often has to be reached *through* the experience of bondage—not apart from it. To put it differently: the higher collectivity is already implied, though latent and unrecognized, in the lower social group. The former operates in a freedom which actually transcends what at the social level we think of as freedom because it actually is a higher form of inevitability or necessity; while what today we call "freedom" is bondage to the dualistic world of alternatives between which the conscious mind and ego-will has to choose after hesitations and inner conflicts. The being who is truly free is he who is beyond choice, because having been *totally and irrevocably* identified with one way of life he simply cannot choose any other way. The Bodhisattva, who has reached a pure spiritual and all-encompassing state of consciousness, cannot *not* be compassionate. He *is* compassion. At a lower level of evolution, the dreamer of utopias whose life is totally consecrated to his great dream, must seek to actualize it. He has really no choice, because he has become the agent of the Neptunian dream. He is the dream-become-act. He is Mary having received the Annunciation; the avataric life within her womb could not be ignored or even less dismissed. Neptune is Mary—or *mare, the sea.* It is the human sea moved ineluctably by galactic winds of destiny. These play havoc with the Saturnian structures of "merely men," men caught in the pressures of the past determining what we call today, and unable to even dream of "tomorrow that sings." [4]

Neptune was discovered when the Industrial Revolution had shown its power to transform simple peasants into proletariat whose lives since childhood had become blighted by wage-slavery. A few visionaries then began to dream utopian dreams of regenerated society pervaded by Christ-love. The dreams, in practically all cases, failed to become lasting realities, yet the vision remains and is now being revived in many ways; and, unsuccessful though it be, it remains and indeed is bound to multiply as a witness to the potentiality of galactic realizations in human natures. Nevertheless, there can be no concrete and lasting realization as long as the deconditioned process in individuals whose consciousness has become illumined by the Neptunian dream has not been thorough and irreversible. It is to this irreversibility that Pluto contributes. It may contribute to the purification in a fanatic and dictatorial manner, leading to one kind or another of totalitarianism; it may also lead to those deepest catharses following which there can be no return to the oppressive and egocentric past.

Neptune has been called the planet of ecstasy, for it refers to what seems to be man's never-ending yearning for that which can take him out of his limited, isolated self and his narrowly defined ego-stance *(ex-stasis).* The Neptunian path may lead us to the unitive state of the true mystic, in which all separating differentiations have ceased or have been forgotten, and all is—or seems to be—"one." Man wishes to forget so many things that bind,

[4] This phrase, once famous, was uttered by a member of the French Underground just before being shot to death and defiantly proclaiming that his death would usher *"les demains qui chantent."*

oppress, or weary him! He has found many ways of doing so. But to forget is not to be free from the temporarily forgotten pressure or solitude. All the drugs men have used since time immemorial, from alcohol to psychedelics, can only provide temporary surcease or illusory liberation. Wherever there is existence there must be duality. All life requires polarization. Unity is a "great dream," if we look for it in the manifested universe. Yet this dream is necessary to polarize and stimulate our existence, if we are to move, step by step, on the path to an ever-higher consciousness and reality—galactic, metagalactic, universal. The term *universe* is revealing, for it means "turned toward unity."

The use of the phrase "unity in diversity" has recently become widespread; it should really be "diversity seeking unity." The many are yearning for the state of oneness; but to speak of a *state* of oneness is to indulge in Neptunian illusion. All that man may reach is a *consciousness* of unity; dualism remains the actual fact, except perhaps at the most metaphysical level. In terms of existence, we should speak of wholeness, not of oneness. Life moves from lesser whole to greater whole, from atom and cells to man and galaxies; and this movement is illumined by the great dream of unity. For everything that moves, unity can only be a great dream, a nonconceptual concept, a "not this, not this. . . ." Even Sankaracharya's most metaphysical system of philosophy spoke of the ultimate condition as *advaita,* which means "nondual"— this is a negative statement. It signifies a dynamic urge to go beyond duality *as duality is being experienced, at any level of existence.* What is implied is a summons to take a step ahead on the path to an ever-wider realization of the wholeness of universal being. No one can ever "reach" unity and remain *one.*

In this sense, unity is an "illusion" (from the Latin, *ludo* "I play") and the universe is the Play of Brahma, the Creative God. But Brahma is not unity; He is only *a* one—the immense One from whom our universe issued in its multiplicity. Nevertheless for whomsoever belongs to the realm of multiplicity. unity is the *necessary* illusion without which there could be no progress, no material or spiritual evolution. Without the incredibly varied forms of glamour which life presents to its living organisms, there could be no reaching beyond the narrow uncreative wholeness of the Saturn-ruled organic unit bound by skeleton and skin. Life's most characteristic glamour is that of sex, or (in the widest sense of sex) of what we call love. Without this glamour, there could be no evolution. The glamour of human love and motherhood makes the perpetuation of the species possible. Neptune is the symbol of glamour—thus of the necessary accompaniment to the process of evolution from lesser to greater whole. What we call "compassion" is also glamour in its highest mode; for the great Compassionate Ones are beings who, having achieved the perfection of their cycles of existence—the threshold of Nirvana—are "glamourized" into refusing this Nirvana and identifying compassionately with the failures and waste products of the cycle. Thus a *higher form of wholeness*—a new universe along the spiral path without conceivable end—may be reached.

The glamour of Christhood! If Christ, as Rudolf Steiner claimed, was a "Solar Archangel," did He not come to redeem mankind and impregnate the Earth with the high vibration of His shed blood, in order that *the transformation of Sun into galactic star* may be accomplished and man may find his consciousness opened to the galactic dimension of existence?

We speak a great deal today of charisma. But what is this mysterious capacity some human beings have to impress and fascinate others if not the ability powerfully to evoke great images that inspire the imagination of people? I once spoke of Neptune as "evocator extraordinary." The Neptunian individual evokes images that have transforming power. Words can be images with transforming power; so are mutating seeds. The whole psychic life of a human being is involved in and moved by images. Modern psychology of the Jungian type—especially as developed by Ira Progoff, and even by Fritz Kunkel and Erik Berne—deals with psychic images. But there are all kinds of images: images that lull to sleep and to aimless dreaming, as well as images that stir to greater action and wider consciousness; images that intoxicate and may even madden the unwary, as well as reveal new forms of order or new values and feelings; images which are concentrates of woe or joy; images which dissolve the ego into the weary death of feelinglessness, or bring an ecstasy that heightens feeling to a pitch of creative intensity.

Our inner life is entirely dependent on images and symbols. Religion uses images as great myths to inspire collectivities; it is an integrated whole of images centered around a highly imaginative Founder whose "eidetic" consciousness is able to encompass the wholeness of existence from a standpoint as yet unattained by most human beings. Images, even more than ideas, rule the world; for, in order to achieve convincing power, a transformative idea has to become clothed in an imagery able to evoke in human beings the near-possibility of new and inspiring developments.

While the Saturnian type of intellectual consciousness deals with concepts linked by logic, the Neptunian type of consciousness is "eidetic" because it is based on often a-logical, and perhaps irrational, sequences of images—images that interpenetrate, images of the dream state, or the state between waking and sleeping. A few modern psychologists make a significant use of *"rêves éveillés"* (waking dreams) which unfold in a state bordering the waking consciousness—a state in which images flow of their own momentum, yet can respond to external or conscious guidance. Such a state is typically Neptunian in its open-endedness and often its confusion and formlessness.

Astrology can also be used in a similar manner, using the birth chart as a means to evoke images in the mind of the person to whom it refers—as Dr. Raaum has done with significant success.[5]

---

[5] One of the strange ideas carelessly accepted by most present-day astrologers is that astrology is ruled by the planet Uranus. Considering the sudden, violent character of Uranian upheavals, such a rulership seems totally unwarranted; while the rather confused and imprecise—because vast and all-inclusive—nature of astrological concepts and symbols, plus the glamourous

Asiatic techniques of meditation often use those complex yet centered images called mandalas in order to stimulate the process of personal integration. The Tarot cards have served similar purposes, evoking archetypal images which have universal meaning for human beings. The Sabian Symbols in astrology constitute a cyclic series of more modern images which can be referred to the factors found in a birth chart, or used as oracular means in a way similar to that offered by the ancient Chinese *I Ching*.[6]

To the man living within a sphere of activity totally bound by Saturn and animated by the energies of Jupiter and Mars—with their inner life polarities, Mercury and Venus—the images evoked by Neptune are a constant challenge to transformation and to the realization of ego- and tradition-transcending values. It is often a subtle challenge whenever Neptunian glamour meets Venusian magnetic attraction, or any Mercurial play with familiar concepts and memories. While the action of Uranus' forces can be referred to "solutions of continuities" and "waterfalls" in the flow of our feelings, thoughts, and behavior, what Neptune evokes is the deep-seated longing for, yet also the awe-inspiring experience of the sea.

All rivers lead to the sea. Everything returns to the vast impassive expanse of oceanic being. We long for this kind of return, once we are no longer yearning for a return to our mother's womb. It may be the same deep desire of the individualized consciousness and the much battered and alienated ego, but it is desire at two widely different levels, and it is unwise to reduce the former

---

fascination they so often exert upon the idealistic and aspiring person, fit very well the character of Neptune.

What happened was that people somehow confused the Muse, Urania, to whom astronomy was attributed, with the great god, Ouranos who was the symbol of undifferentiated and universal space before the appearance of Saturn and Jupiter, who dethroned him. The modern Uranus has no direct relationship with the mythological Ouranos—unless we associated Ouranos with the Galaxy, of which Uranus is only an agent. Yet such an association would betray the essential meaning of the Greek cosmological myth.

[6] Cf. Rudhyar, *An Astrological Mandala: The Cycle of Transformation and Its 360 Symbolic Phases* (New York: Random House, 1973, hardbound and paperback).

to the latter. If we do it, as a reductionistic type of psychology has done with unfortunate results for a couple of generations of Western individuals, it is because we have refused to accept the possibility of rising above the level of a disintegrating and fundamentally disruptive society that proclaimed in words Neptunian ideals which it disregarded in everyday practice—a society rather well symbolized today by the tragicomedy of Watergate, duplicating any number of similar, though less publicized forms of hypocritical behavior.

It is against such situations that Pluto acts with relentless vigor; and it seems to do so particularly well when—as it does today—Pluto matches Neptune's speed in the solar system and penetrates Neptune's orbit, causing havoc with glamour and myths—even perhaps the glamour of living and the myth of death.

·4·

Pluto and the Experience of Depth, Void, and Recentering

Many astrologers see in Pluto a symbol of materialism or a destructive and disintegrative power at work. Superficially they are correct, at least in the majority of present-day situations. Yet such an interpretation fails to reveal the essential character of the complex, universal process symbolized by the planet announced and discovered this century by American astronomers. This process releases what is required in order to *reduce to essentials* whatever has reached the end of a cycle; and the end of a cycle is also the moment at which reintegration as part of a larger cycle may occur. Pluto deals therefore with *the possibility of rebirth*; and obviously this implies the experience of what, for people of narrow understanding, tends to take the form of "death."

Pluto does not insure rebirth. It simply refers to the *prerequisites* of rebirth, one of which is what we witness as a dying body, or as the psychomental disintegration of a personality or a whole culture. Pluto is not concerned with what the process may lead to. It does not deal with end results, only with what must be passed *through* if a fundamental kind of results are to be produced as the necessary foundation for a new life at a higher—or in tragic cases, lower—level of the spiral of evolution. Pluto, I believe, does not produce such a foundation; this should refer to the symbolic activity of a trans-Plutonian planet, which I have tentatively baptized Proserpine. But the possibility of such a foundation is implied in Pluto's action; indeed it gives to whatever Pluto represents in a person's or a nation's life its true and essential purpose.

In the light of such an astrological understanding of Pluto's function, we can piece together the various parts of the puzzle that this planet presents to the minds of not a few students of astrology. We can also dismiss most of the radically negative statements made about Pluto, seeing them as relatively biased interpretations which can do a great deal of psychological harm when incorporated in the interpretation of a person's birth chart.

It should be clear, nevertheless, that there is in Pluto's countenance and its astrological effects much that is awesome and relentless, often also totally ruthless in an impersonal and "karmic" manner. Yet Pluto operates quite differently from Saturn, which has often been considered the symbol of karma at work. Saturnian karma works in a rather precise and automatic manner, somewhat according to the old formula: "An eye for an eye, a tooth for a tooth." What is implied in such karmic workings can also be stated in terms of the cosmic principle of universal harmony. Anything that generates a leftward disequilibrium has automatically to be balanced—in time and space—by a rightward action, and vice versa.

If the person experiencing the karmic consequences of previous acts learns from these experiences, this is fine; but the karmic force does not care. A society which punishes the criminal according to a fixed law with an impersonal character is normally unconcerned with what the punishment does to the person who broke the law and was caught doing it. For this reason justice is said to be "blind." Rare are the cases where a "punishment" is meted purposely to create a controlled situation providing a deep catharsis and the possibility of moral and social rebirth—even though the concept of justice may today be hesitantly and in-equally evolving in that direction. When it does, it tries to embody the Plutonian spirit.

Saturn, let us not forget, has a character that is bound up with that of a solar autocrat—or, as a substitute, a rigid, traditional legal code, such as the Napoleonic code. Saturn refers to the justice of an absolute king who cannot accept challenges to his power and can bear even less to see his laws scorned; except in the rare cases in which it pleases him to show—or for devious rea-sons he is pressured into showing—his magnanimity, and he pardons the offender. On the other hand, Pluto never "pardons," because he does not "punish" or automatically exacts payment proportionate to the offense. Pluto registers the fact that a time has come for the possibility to move from one level of conscious-ness and activity to another; he then produces the conditions re-quired for such a passage or transmutation.

The more bound the consciousness is to Saturnian patterns and memories, the harsher these conditions. If Uranus and Neptune have not succeeded in giving a good start to the process of trans-formation, Pluto can indeed be ruthless as well as relentless. If, on the other hand, the Uranian and Neptunian forces have done their transforming work, and the individual has accepted their message and readied himself for the final "descent into hell"— the Dark Night of the Soul—he may with calm strength meet the Plutonian process of total denudation and the void to which it leads. Such a person already carries in his heart the vision of the New Life and no longer resists the transformation, whose purpose he has consciously made his own. Punishment has become purga-tion—the breaking down of obstacles to the flow of spiritual power within his total being, or at least as much of the total being as can stand the inrush without being shattered by the galactic energy.

The action of karma may be involved, but a karmic retribution which is totally accepted and given the meaning of a liberation from past conscious and unconscious memories ceases to be

Saturnian; it becomes the token one has to pay for entrance into the galactic realm of spiritual consciousness. In extreme emotional cases we have the joyous ecstasy of the martyrs singing while being tortured, because they know uncontrovertibly that this is the way to absolute union with the Divine Beloved, the Avatar.

In the symbolism of Christ's descent to hell for three days after his Crucifixion, we see a particularly significant example of Plutonian activity, for the development of galactic consciousness requires a total experience of the meaning that disintegration and failure have had during the cycle in which one has attained the Christlike state of consciousness. Everything that has been part of this cycle must be encompassed by the consciousness which now has a totally holistic and thus eonic or divine character. The White Adept in some way must have become aware of, and have empathetically felt the tragic state of the Black Adept, because in his compassion he includes the darkness as well as the light. He can no longer hate or feel horror for evil, because for the supreme Good there is no evil, but only the shadow of the divine Light upon the unredeemed memory of the ancient past. But it must be truly the supreme Good indisputably revealing its nature in total, impersonal compassion, and not the little good encapsuled in man's pale social or religious virtues!

The fact that the Crucifixion and its aftermath, the three days "descent to hell" are celebrated at the time of the vernal equinox is deeply significant; for that moment of the year's cycle refers, at least symbolically, to the process of germination; and *germination is the crucifixion of the seed.* Out of the torn seed the first thing to emerge is the rootlet, and this rootlet "descends" into the humus, *produce of the decay of leaves and of all that once had been living.* The dark soil is the hell of the life-sphere, but it is also the foundation of all living processes—the "dark mother" which is the past, who will be redeemed as her decayed materials are drawn upward toward air and light within the new life and eventually reach the flower state.

Germination is a Plutonian process, and this is why in astrology

Pluto should "rule" Aries, the vernal equinox sign of the zodiac, symbol of the creative impulse which initiates all new life-processes. However, Pluto is *associated* with Aries rather than ruling it; for the concept of rulership breaks down entirely when we realize that the trans-Saturnian planets are *in* the solar system, but not *of* it. This concept was entirely valid in the Ptolemaic Sun-to-Saturn world, for it expressed a profound philosophy of life. It no longer should be applied to a heliocosm in which the Sun is primarily understood to be a star, one among billions, within the vast cosmic organism of the Galaxy. All that can be said is that in the new galactic approach to the planets and to the zodiac— the *tropical* zodiac which is the background on which we plot the cyclically changing relationship of the Earth to the Sun—the signs following Capricorn (the apex of Saturn's power) correspond to the basic phases in the process of transformation symbolized by Uranus, Neptune, and Pluto. Thus Uranus is associated with Aquarius, Neptune with Pisces, Pluto with Aries, and an assumed Proserpine with Taurus.

Pluto, however, is the challenger of all that Mars represents in the Sun-to-Saturn system. Pluto's impersonality challenges Mars' essentially personal-emotional character. The challenges occur in Scorpio as well as in Aries, just as Neptune's challenge to Jupiter occurs in Pisces (symbol of the last moment of a cultural cycle) as well as in Sagittarius (which represents the achievement by a culture of its fundamental philosophical and legal character); and Uranus challenges Saturn in Capricorn as well as in Aquarius, for the moment the days begin to lengthen, the power of Saturn is doomed, even at the very apex of its power.

All challenges by the planets that are agents of the Galaxy are inherently causes of suffering for the consciousness immured within Saturnian patterns; but the acceptance of suffering is an essential part of the process of transformation. The "descent to hell" is, in a sense, a dramatization of the inevitability of suffering in such a process. More generally still, wherever there is the experience of depth there inevitably is a concomitant experience of suffering. But, in our global world, the direction of depth leads us to center; and the experience of center is essential to spiritual development. All centers—be they those of atoms, cells, suns, or galaxies—are not only related in the fourth dimension of "interpenetration," they actually are one in what one might call the fifth dimension. This is the ancient Hindu concept of the identity of the individual atman and the universal Brahman, reflected in the yogic salutation "I am Thou" that evokes the feeling of an essential identity of the centers in all human beings. I should add that such a salutation distinguishes the Hindu from the Hebraic-Christian type of spirituality, because the latter instead speaks of "I *and* Thou" (cf. Buber's famous book with that title), replacing identification with a "dialogue" between essentially different entities—a dialogue which at the limit is one that relates God the Creator to man, the creature.

What we can broadly call depth-psychology aims, in its most significant aspect, at giving to human consciousness the experience of depth—and in some instance (especially with Carl Jung and Assagioli) the experience of center. The process of "individuation" which constitutes the main topic in Jungian psychotherapy and in psychosynthesis should lead not only to an experience of centering—for the personal ego is also the center of the Saturn-bounded field of consciousness—but to the transfer of the center from the essentially limited and temporary ego-field to the vaster and permanent realm of "the Self." The latter is not only a vaster field, because it encompasses both the conscious and the unconscious areas of the total psyche, but a qualitatively different field. It has the quality of inclusiveness in contrast to the basic exclusivism of the ego-dominated consciousness.

Mars arouses and focuses the soli-lunar energies of the personality in the direction of an emotionally desired goal. It represents a going out into the world of the surface of the globe, the biosphere. It involves a more or less "horizontal" spreading of energy in terms of a relationship with some object; a relationship which may be negative, thus a fleeing from that object. Pluto, on the contrary, essentially refers to the focusing of the power (or the activity) of some kind of "group" (concrete or transcendental) upon and through an individual who finds himself invested with that power, a power expressing or seeking a centering purpose. To Mars' intensely personal action, Pluto answers with a collective urge for activity, a collective urge seeking a mind or a will that, by giving it a conscious focus, will provide a center from which the purpose may be disseminated.

At the highest level Pluto serves to focus galactic energies upon mankind *through* individuals ready undeviatingly to assume a role of destiny; and in that sense Pluto's action is "vertical," not "horizontal." At a social-cultural level Pluto represents the deep-seated urge in a collectivity—a nation, a social group, a profession —to formulate *through* especially gifted persons the characteristic quality ("style" or way of life) of the historical stage of evolution at which the group or the nation operates. While Neptune represents the general pressure of a collectivity upon the individuals which it includes—and thus, for instance, signifies the individual's subservience to fashion and propaganda of all types—Pluto in a birth chart indicates *the possibility* for a person to become the active mouthpiece of the group's spirit through positive, creative action.

This Plutonian focusing of social or biological energies upon an individual who is able to express the group's character and purpose often results in what appears to be actions imbued with personal ambition or self-gratification; yet behind this personal façade a wider kind of unconscious or semiconscious motivation operates. For instance, at the psychological level the emotional attraction between a young man and woman ordinarily takes apparently personal and possessive forms; yet behind this appearance it is the human species, and often the culture or religion of the youths, which impel or compel them to mate. On the surface everything seems personal and Martian, but in the unconscious depths of the two young people it is the collective purpose of the race or the culture which seeks expression. Any focusing of generic or social energy and purpose through the actions of individuals, often unaware of what impels them to act, is Plutonian.[1]

This Plutonian challenge to Mars archetypically occurs in Aries. Life itself, in its generic sense, is the real actor in all cosmic or racial beginnings. This is what, in the most ancient mythologies, the great god Eros (or *Kama deva* in India) meant; only much later was this primal force of universal life reduced to the "human, all too human" character it occupies in popular conceptions and familiar language (witness the common use of the term, erotic). In early days the Greek Eros and the Hindu *Kama deva* were the firstborn among the gods. They represented the cosmic desire to create a new world; and such desire inevitably implies a "descent" into chaos. Chaos represents the undifferentiated primeval condition of matter, the residua of extinct forms of energy, the "dark soil" or dust of past universes. Every creative activity in its essential character is a descent into matter. The *universal* One in Its diffuse and undifferentiated state, spreads out in infinite Space, seeks to focus itself into a *particular* one, the source of a new manifestation; and to do that it must become centered in matter. We interpret this action symbolically by speaking of a "descent" into the depths and the darkness. All such descents are motivated by a desire for new and more inclusive experiences in some form of life, at whatever level these forms are envisioned as containers or expressions of a cosmic (micro- or macrocosmic) process.

At the level of our present Western society and, in a more general sense, of what the Hindu philosopher called Kali Yuga (the Greek Iron Age, the Age of the Dark Mother, Kali), Plutonian descents have a tragic character, for individuals and nations have always to meet many dark and fear-full memories. These

---

[1] In this sense a police force is a manifestation of Plutonian power at the social (and at times, political) power. The policeman who abuses his power commits a greater crime than a mere individual who injures another individual—a Martian act. Yet in our illegal society, he is most often only reprimanded or dismissed. The abuse or misuse of collective power invested upon a man should be the greatest crime a person can commit.

memories have to be met in the underground darkness if there
is to be new and creative beginnings. This is, in Jungian terms,
the meeting with the Shadow. Nevertheless if this meeting is
courageously and unfalteringly experienced, the Shadow is transformed into God-in-the-depth, the God of the mysteries, the
"living" God who polarizes God-in-the-highest, and thus reveals
the essential unity of matter and spirit, and also of failure and
success—or better still the changeless, all-encompassing, and ineffable Harmony of Non-being and Being, or Potentiality and
Actuality.[2]

In most fairy tales, the ugly Beast seeking love is transformed
into the radiant Prince, once the maiden is able to feel in her
heart compassion for the deformed ugliness. In Greek esoteric
mythology Pluto is not only ruler of the Underground, but also
the symbol of abundance and wealth. It is symbolized also by "the
Pearl of great price" which, hidden within the viscous shell-en-
closed substance of the oyster, can only be found by the daring
diver into the sea-depths of the unconscious; and, in order to
succeed in his quest, the diver must develop a large lung-capacity
for breathing—the breath symbolizing the most essential aspect of
the process of spiritual realization. Pearls are produced by the
oyster after some irritating substance has been introduced into its
seemingly shell-secure living space. Suffering is necessary if some
degree of transmutation and transsubstantiation is to be experienced; but all depends on the attitude toward suffering and
pain. Tragedy must be accepted. It must be *understood*; and to
understand is not only to "stand under" and bear the full weight
of what is understood, thus experiencing all its mass and its contents; it is also to become aware of the purpose of the burden
placed upon one's shoulders—the purpose this burden and the
experience of it have within the large cycle of one's existence, and
if possible of mankind's and the world's existence.

Pluto, more than any other planet, can lead to the reality of
what is often too glibly called "cosmic consciousness"; but it

2 Cf. *The Planetarization of Consciousness*, Chap. 5.

certainly does not need to do so. The Shadow has most subtle ways of hiding the reality under various forms of Neptunian glamour. As already stated, Pluto's action is largely conditioned by what a person's response to Uranian and Neptunian forces and events has been. The Uranian revolutionist can easily be thrown off his course by the intensity of his passion for violently tearing down oppressive factors and accepting no compromise; the Neptunian idealist may be misled by the glamour of pseudomystical experiences which make him lose his way in a heavy, even if iridescent, mist; and the Neptunian humanitarian may sink in the quicksand of sentimentality. What is taken for cosmic consciousness may only be a *feeling*-experience, instead of a clear realization of the cosmic-divine Mind in its impersonal and unerring cyclic operations—what Sri Aurobindo calls the Supermind, or even the higher aspect of the Overmind.

A significant and contrasting relationship can be made between Pluto and Mercury. Mercury symbolizes the mind at the stage in which its operations are conditioned by the need of the life organism for survival, expansion, and reproduction, and by the social-cultural ambitions of the ego. On the other hand, Pluto stands for the totally impersonal cosmic Mind—the Mind that deals with universal principles and archetypes, the holistic and eonic Mind. At a lower level, it refers to the style of an epoch, rather than the personal contribution of a particular artist or writer, very often appreciated at first for his superficial and supposedly "original" characteristics. For this reason, Pluto's position in one of the Houses of a birth chart reveals the type of experience through which a person will most fruitfully contribute to the style of his or her time; and as we will presently see, Pluto's position in a particular zodiacal sign gives a basic clue to the life style of a generation.

Summing up the foregoing, we find that the most fundamental meaning of all Plutonian processes is that they force us, often relentlessly, to devaluate or abandon all that is a manifestation of *surface* living and to plumb as profound a depth of human experience as our mental, affective, and spiritual condition can withstand. Surface living can be interpreted at the social-cultural level in terms of our habitual and taken-for-granted responses to the behavior and feeling patterns of our society or class. At a more personal level, Pluto represents, as we have already seen, all forms of depth-psychology; thus any determined attempt to discover our "fundamental nature"—in the sense in which Zen philosophy uses these words.

Pluto can also be said to lead human minds to a realization that a central core of "great verities" exists underneath the variety of religious beliefs and practices. Theosophists refer to it as "the universal Wisdom-Religion." All the institutionalized cults which, in their external and popular aspects, have ever sought to meet the local and relatively temporary needs of particular human collectivities in various regions of the earth-surface, are derived from it. It is based on what is essential in human nature.

In this sense, Pluto is the planet most closely related to true Occultism—whether in its constructive or destructive forms (i.e., White or Black adeptship)—not only because true Occultism teaches us how to operate within the realm of *forces* (the astromental world), of which material bodies are only the externalized manifestations, but also because it claims that all basic human knowledge came to nascent mankind through an "Original Revelation" bestowed by extraterrestrial Beings who were the "seed" of a previous planetary cycle, and that this knowledge, in its pure condition, remains the possession of Occult Brotherhoods still existing today. With the assistance of some of the individual members of these hidden Brotherhoods, man can become attuned to their collective Minds; but such an attunement, and in rare cases eventual identification, can only be achieved through an arduous and dangerous approach to the ultimate realities of existence, the Path of Initiation. Pluto rules over that Path with absolute rigor and in terms of unvarying and impersonal laws embodying cosmic principles.

Occultism in its true character (which has practically nothing to do with what is today popularly known as Occultism) is *cosmic depth-psychology*. It can only be significantly understood and constructively applied by individuals who have been made inwardly "separate" from the mass-vibration of mankind (and in general of the Earth's biosphere) by Uranian visitations and deepseated crises, and who have experienced Neptunian expansion of consciousness *and of feeling* without being lured into fascinating bypaths by the protean glamour surrounding the occult Path.

It should be clear that the occult way is not the devotional way, and much that passes for mysticism belongs to another line of approach, even though every "white" occultist must have had transforming and illuminating mystical experiences. The relationship between true Mysticism and Occultism can be symbolized by that between Neptune and Pluto. I have already mentioned the fact that there are times when Pluto comes closer to the Sun than Neptune ever does and thus can be said to operate during these times within Neptune's orbit. We are today very near such a period, which lasts about twenty years. These periods often witness a repolarization of the collective consciousness and the ideals of mankind along lines which, in one way or another, stress factors deeply rooted in human nature and thus common to at least a large section of mankind. In 1942, Vice-President Henry Wallace said that "the century on which we are emerging—the century which will come out of this war—can be and must be the century of the common man." Such a century actually began with the great Depression of 1929 and the following years, at which time Pluto was discovered. In my book *The Faith That Gives Meaning to Victory* (Fall, 1942), I pointed out that Henry Wallace should have referred not so much to "the common man" as to *man's common humanity,* and I added that:

> As long as individuals glory in that they are different from others and identify themselves exclusively with their differences, there can be no peace on earth. Peace and union will

come when individuals will know themselves *first* as humans,
then as individuals; when individuals will be willing to con-
secrate their differentiated gifts and faculties to the welfare of
humanity; when the egocentric personalities of our day will
realize, to use the beautiful words of St. Exupery in his *Flight
to Arras,* that "The individual is a path; *Man* only matters,
who takes that path" (p. 15). . . . The individual is rooted in
man's common humanity, whether he admits it or not, whether
he likes it or not. . . . Behind his will and his power is the great
tide of human evolution, which sweeps on and ultimately ful-
fills its inherent goal—merely modified, delayed or accelerated
by the individual will of separate men. Surely the individual
is the supreme flowering of that human evolution; surely the
great genius stands as the guiding light and the creator. *But
what is it that is power within him?* . . . Power is welling up
constantly from the common humanity and the common structures (an individual) shares with all men (pp. 17–18).

The compelling potency, the vivid realization, and the depth-
experience of this common humanity are Plutonian factors. Sex
has become so glorified in this "century of the common man" because sexual interaction is one of the most basic ways of obtain-
ing such a depth-experience of the power embodied in all human
organisms. Wilhelm Reich and the bioenergetic enthusiasts place
this Plutonian experience at the center of all human living. This
experience undertones all personal distinctions and scorns racial-
cultural classifications and prejudices. It is the experience of "life"
in its impersonal, or rather *subpersonal,* manifestation as sex and
orgastic energy. Man's common humanity does not "transcend"
the individualized achievements of a culture and of beings refined
by such a culture; for, in order to experience it, the individual
has to "descend" into the common and the undifferentiated. It is
a Plutonian descent. If at times it turns out to be a descent into
hell, it is because, in our present humanity and for immense
periods of time, the sexual function has been perverted by the
ego-will seeking to use the life force of the biosphere for self-en-
joyment and power. This has been the fateful result of the process

of individualization which differentiates man from animals. In this sense, Pluto forces individualized and "civilized" men and women to descend not only to the level at which the animal power of life dominates, but below it.

Sex is not the only manifestation of that level of activity and consciousness. All rituals, bringing together a relatively large number of people to a state of mass-feeling and behavior in which they act as an emotional undifferentiated crowd, seek to arouse the power of man's common humanity. They are Plutonian instrumentalities, especially whenever they operate in a nation which otherwise seeks to foster and takes pride in the individualism of its citizens; for in such cases there is no deeply effective Saturnian power to set traditional limits to the behavior of what has become a totally irrational and uncontrollable mob. Religious rites, and at the socioeconomic level, the equally ritualistic practices of business, operate within the Saturnian boundaries of a tradition, which also—at least in some cultures—imposed specific forms to sexual activity. It is when these Saturnian forms break down under the onslaught of Uranian forces, or have been rendered meaningless and boring by a newly aroused Neptunian feeling of totally open communality and boundlessness, that what was until then a ritual becomes a Plutonian mob scene or an orgy.

The Freudian type of psychological "reductionism"—that is, the teaching that the more differentiated and conscious manifestations of idealism, religion, and artistic genius can be reduced to the operation of pressures, obstacles, or disturbances in the flow of the life energy (*libido* and sex)—is a typical Plutonian process particularly acting upon the easily distorted or blocked Mars function in human individuals; and Freud's birth chart places a striking emphasis on a lonely retrograde Mars. It is true, however, that the flowering of plants above the surface of the soil depends upon the health of the roots in the depth and the dark of what, psychologically speaking, is symbolized by the subconscious or personal unconscious. What until now we have known as "culture" is deeply bound to, or at least basically conditioned by local geographical and climatic factors—thus Sun-Saturn factors. This is the surface-realm of man's potential of being. A *global* realization of the ideal condition of "civilization"—the Holy City, the New Jerusalem, etc.—will be actualized when its archetypal outlines and the principles determining its structure will have been revealed by the higher galactic manifestations of Pluto.

Many years ago I wrote an article entitled "Neptune, the Sea—Pluto, the Globe." The globe contains the sea, and while the latter is vast, profound, and mysterious, it has no center. A globe is centered. It is a three-dimensional mandala. Neptune is not only the sea, but also the atmospheric ocean which permeates every living organism through the breathing process—a subtler type of sea, having also its powerful and at times devastating storms. The two oceans—water and air—envelope the realm where continents give birth to human cultures; but oceans and land obey Plutonian gravitation, *the pull to center.*

Such a pull leads to integration; and, in a sense, Pluto is the ultimate Integrator. Yet there are premature types of integration, and integrative processes born of the fear of Neptunian chaos. Such processes have led mankind to such developments as Neoclassicism or Neoscholasticism in the arts [3]—totalitarian Fascism and Nazism in politics—and in the world of city tenements, the gangs, the Mafia, and other more or less criminal and coercive agglomerations of frustrated and/or bewildered individuals seeking power in cohesive and leader-ruled activity.

On the other hand, when strongly unified groups emerge out of the natural evolutionary process of social growth, they operate under a Saturnian principle; we have a rationalistic and formalistic "classical" system, such as Europe has seen in the seventeenth and early eighteenth centuries. (Louis XIV, king by "divine right"

[3] In music we had Stravinsky, the originator of Neoclassicism after his powerful *The Rite of Spring* and the Communist Revolution in Russia which made of him an exile; and Schoenberg, who transformed post-Wagnerian chromaticism into a rigidly formalistic and intellectually scholastic atonalism with its twelve-tone system.

and the Versailles castle are outstanding symbols of such a development.)

Neoclassicism, like Mussolini-style totalitarianism, emerges compulsively *after* a period of relative Neptunian chaos and is powered by a collective fear of the results of such a chaotic interlude. These retrogressive ("return to . . .") movements cannot accept the fact that chaos can be the beginning of the gestation of a new and more encompassing order. Their operation could perhaps be symbolized by a regressive Pluto; but this does not mean that, in natal astrology, a "retrograde" Pluto in a chart represents a trend toward some form of frightened totalitarianism. Pluto is too often found retrograde in a birth chart for such a conclusion to be at all valid. All that can be said is that a retrograde Pluto evokes the possibility of using fear-reactions as lines of least resistance when the individual is confronted with what seems to be disturbingly chaotic situations. It may be considered a warning that, when facing such situations, it may be wiser for the person quietly to return to basic root-experiences rather than plunge overconfidently or naïvely into a tempestuous Neptunian sea. Not every person is innately structured to be a pioneer in inherently dangerous adventures; and the spiritual Path *can be* a dangerous adventure involving extremely serious risks. In the long run, even relative failure may be transformed into more spectacular success; but it can be a *long* run!

Pluto can be seen, at least at the present time, as Guardian of the Threshold which eventually opens up into the starry world of the Galaxy. The Guardian's countenance is often frightening; yet it only reflects our ancient sins of omission as well as commission, our failure to act when the cyclic time had come to move forward, our fears, and our usually well-hidden guilt. Occult stories—like Bulwer Litton's classic novel *Zanoni*, written in the last century—have at times vividly depicted the tragic meeting of an ambitious aspirant with the awesome Guardian.

Whenever an astrologer gives entirely negative characteristics to Pluto, one may well wonder whether he or she does not unconsciously portray the features which the Guardian of the Threshold would present to his or her advance. It is easy to glorify Neptune and the seemingly boundless and rapturous glow of diffuse spirituality and pseudomysticism while linking Pluto to all forms of materialism and dictatorship; it is much harder to face a Pluto that merely reflects one's own hidden face and fully to accept karmic confrontation. One can only go *through* karma by fulfilling it, while holding within one's heart the vision of the future—the realization that one essentially is a star in the Galaxy. To hold securely and unwaveringly such a realization while battered by Plutonian earthquakes is not easy. This nevertheless is the true Plutonian challenge. No one who shrinks before the challenge can spiritually reach his highest goal, his star.

Courage is needed and that will which transcends the puny decisions of the ego and manifests the character of inevitability. No individual should attempt to tread the Path unless he or she *has to,* by virtue of an ineluctable impulsion that cannot be ignored. Once he has begun the journey, he should never stop or look back. He must allow Uranus unceasingly to shatter his cherished limitations, Neptune to expand his consciousness, and Pluto to lead him through darkness into the Void where a new center of light eventually will shine, reorganizing the scattered fragments of what for so long he had accepted as himself.

PART TWO

·5·

The Trans-Saturnian Planets in Zodiacal Signs

So much has been written about what the zodiac represents that there is no need to go into a detailed discussion of it here. I have stated in various books the basic reasons why I do not accept the sidereal zodiac which is supposed to refer to constellations of actual stars. I nevertheless realize that in ancient times, when astrology was locality-centered, when the Earth was believed to be flat, and when astrologers watched directly the dome of the sky, the zodiac referred to star groups through which the Sun passed during its annual journey across the firmament.[1] Astrology in India has significantly retained such an approach, because of the Hindu worship of ancient doctrines, and the lives of human beings become attuned to whatever their culture and tradition considers to be unquestionable truths and facts of existence.

Once the Earth was seen to be one of several planets revolving around an all-powerful Sun, the tropical zodiac became an unavoidable fact of existence, for the changing relationship between the Earth and the Sun had then become the fundamental factor

[1] Cf. *The Astrological Houses.*

in astrology. This relationship was projected upon the sky, forming the tropical zodiac. The twelve equal zodiacal signs represent in modern astronomy and astrology 30-degree segments of the Earth's orbit, also called the ecliptic.

If we were to speak of a truly sidereal zodiac, referring to actual stars, it would be logical to see it from the Sun's point of view, thus *heliocentrically.* In a galactic type of astrology it probably would be best to consider the intersection of the plane of the Sun's equator with the galactic plane as establishing an axis—which in turn provides us with a starting point for a solar (heliocentric) "zodiac." Yet as we would then have reached a galactic point of view, it is highly questionable whether the very concept of zodiac would have any meaning. We would be dealing with the immense period of revolution of the Sun around the galactic center— some 200 million years—and so far we know nothing about what such a period signifies in the Sun's existence. Today there are still astrologers who profess to believe that the Sun not only circles around the Galaxy, but that it also revolves in a much shorter time around some galactic star, which in turn revolves around the galactic center; yet hardly any contemporary astronomer endorses such a belief.

The zodiac should be considered a strictly terrestrial and geocentric concept. It is a frame of reference for an astrological study of what takes place in the solar system insofar as we are affected by it. At any moment, the overall structure of the heliocosm first affects the Sun and its radiations; and these in turn affect the Earth and all organisms living in the biosphere. But as the Earth moves within the field of this heliocosm, it is also directly affected by the very complex situation produced by all the planets moving in a charged solar and galactic field. These two effects are electromagnetic and gravitational; they probably also operate at the level of energies or mind-processes (whatever these might be) which transcend the modes of energy-release we know at present.

In other words, the total situation is so complex and so filled with unknowns that it would seem unwise even to consider the astrological influence attributed to separate planets as explainable in strictly "scientific" terms. It is for this reason that I cannot think of astrology except as a symbolic language, and, in the original and deepest meaning of the term, as a "myth," or *mythos*. We need such a *mythos* in order to have the order of the universe conveyed to our consciousness, and the concept of a galactic dimension is essential for bringing to modern man's attention the existence of transformative and transcendent forces at work.

Myths are necessary to the development of a culture and of the type of consciousness to which they give a specific structure. Just as American democracy has to believe that "all men are created free and equal"—a myth, indeed, if we look at existential facts—in order to maintain at least an ideal orientation toward a transcendent spiritual reality; so the astrologer, if he is consistent and intellectually honest, should accept as a postulate the existence in the universe of a factor X that seeks to impress upon all living organisms a transcendent sense of cosmic order.

Such a sense of order is particularly essential to the specific type of "reflective consciousness" (Teilhard de Chardin) which we call human. At our present stage of evolution it appears logical and valid to speak of this X factor as being "galactic," and possibly implied in the activity of the center of our Galaxy, though, as we shall presently see, such a center does not seem to be what we usually think of as a material mass of substance.

The planets operating between the Sun and Saturn give us definite information as to what this universal order is at the level of the heliocosm—a Saturn-bounded level of consciousness. The planets moving outside the orbit of Saturn indicate to us how the transition between a heliocosmic and a galactic type of consciousness can most significantly be made. They alert us to pitfalls and crises on the way; and, in the charts of individuals, their transits reveal when a general type of change can be expected during the individual's life. However, they do *not* indicate precisely and inevitably the concrete events that will spark such changes; nor do they tell us *how* the person will react or respond to them, and there is a great difference between "reacting" to an event—any living organism or even a molecule does this—and "giving a response" to what it makes *possible*. A response—in the precise sense of the term—can only come from the individualized center of the consciousness, the ego, or the self.

In their transits, the trans-Saturnian planets take several years to move through a zodiacal sign. Uranus takes about seven years; Neptune, twelve to thirteen years; Pluto, a greatly varying period lasting from about twelve to thirty years, because of the unusual elongation of its orbit. It should be evident therefore that the mere fact that a person is born with Neptune or Pluto in a zodiacal sign tells relatively little concerning the person's individual character, vocation, or destiny. It refers only to collective trends; thus, to the character of the generation in which the individual is born. Yet, unfortunately, numerous astrologers and even well-known textbooks state that being born with Neptune or Uranus in Leo or Libra gives a person definite characteristics of a *personal* nature. These characteristics, when at all validly formulated, can only apply to a very large group of persons. They suggest a characteristic life style, and more specifically the way people born within a more or less extended period approach the problem of individual or collective transformation—*if* they consciously or even half-consciously faced such a problem. The position of the planets in natal House indicates in most cases an individual's response to the collective life style and the type of experiences which are most likely to significantly affect his or her consciousness and behavior.

The trans-Saturnian planets act collectively as agents of the Galaxy seeking to dis-Saturnize, and in a sense, dissolarize, man's consciousness, whenever such a consciousness has reached a level at which this alchemical operation is possible. When it is not at all possible, these distant planets simpy do not operate—and they are unknown to man. The fact that they were discovered within the last two hundred years shows that this galactically conditioned liberation and transmutation *is* now possible in a broad collective sense. Before that time, it was possible only under very special conditions and in secret. This is a basic historical fact that every human mind unavoidably interprets in its own way, or rather according to one of several schools of thought. What is presented here is an astrological interpretation relating the spiritual, psychic, and social pressures under which we are laboring to a broad cosmic picture. On such a picture a new *mythos* can be built which could inspire human collectivities during what appears to be a critical period of changes ahead of us. The recent growth in the popularity of astrology suggests that mankind is susceptible to the influence of such a great cosmic myth. It is important to emphasize that facts are not opposed to myths, for any valid and consciousness-transforming myth is based on actual facts experienced by at least some human beings. The myth extends these facts to make them not only the common property of mankind, or at least of a whole culture, but a common and fascinating incentive for us to take the next step in human evolution.

Thus far we have considered mainly the manner in which an individual, or a particular group of persons, emerges from the Saturnian realm of egocentric existence into the no-man's land through which the Path of Transformation winds its tortuous way. Uranus came first, then Neptune, and last Pluto—and probably the as-yet-unknown Proserpine. But when we deal with collective and historical situations we should realize that the Galaxy acts through Pluto, Neptune, and Uranus in a "descending" order, i.e., from the universal to the particular. Pluto then produces the more basic keynote. Neptune and Uranus develop further, in different ways, what Pluto sounded out. I shall therefore begin with Pluto as I attempt to define in broad terms what seems most characteristically to be aroused by the position of the three trans-Saturnian in zodiacal signs. Since the zodiac refers to the relationship of the Earth to the Sun, zodiacal positions are simply the normal astrological way of indicating how planets are related to both the Earth and the Sun. Or we might say that they indicate the geocentric possibility of response to what the planet at that time brings to the entire solar system.

Pluto in Zodiacal Signs

When Pluto was finally identified on February 18, 1930, by C. W. Tombaugh at the Lowell Observatory in Flagstaff, Arizona, it had reached the 18th degree of Cancer. It was retrograde and near its North Node, then on the 20th degree. I shall begin with that zodiacal sign because, for our present humanity, it marks the focus of the transforming process as it was brought to the conscious collective level. The famous Wall Street crash had occurred only a few months before and the great Depression was beginning. The Sabian Symbol for this 18th degree is significant: *"a hen scratching the ground to find nourishment for her progeny:* The personal concern with everyday nourishment necessary to sustain one's outreaching activities. . . . A person has to feed (his symbolic children) with social substance gathered from the 'ground' of his community." [2] We may remember what was said some pages back concerning the relation of Pluto to the decaying humus and what it contains, including seeds. And, for millions of people, 1930 and the following years were indeed filled with the problem of feeding themselves and their families.

Pluto in CANCER (July 1913 to August 1938) [3]

Cancer is the sign of personality integration at the level of traditional or ego-consciousness—integration for the purpose of survival in any environment in which survival is possible. It is a sign therefore ruled by the Moon which represents the capacity for adjustment to external conditions, an adjustment or adapta-

[2] Cf. *An Astrological Mandala.*

[3] Because all distant planets move back and forth in the zodiac, the time at which they can be said to enter a new sign is only approximate. It would actually be better to use the heliocentric ingress in the sign, that is, the time when a planet enters a sign in terms of its heliocentric position.

tion aiming at optimum organic well-being. Cancer is related to the mother and the home life, *if* such a life is a bulwark against chaos and social pressures, and the mother teaches the child by her example how to develop an effective capacity for adaptation to the condition of life in society and in nature.

What Pluto, appearing in the midst of Cancer, was trying to convey to mankind was therefore that the home and family situation had to be radically transformed. The outer circumstances were such that this message was impressed in a relentless and impressive manner; yet how few have understood it! These circumstances were largely the result of the Industrial Revolution which began to produce inescapable results when Pluto was located in the sign Aries from 1822 to 1851; but the entrance of Pluto into Cancer marked the Balkan prelude to World War I, and therefore the definite breakdown of the old social order in Europe and, by reaction, in the United States and all over the world. The Russian Revolution occurred during the transit of Pluto, and the basic patterns of human society were subject to a drastic upheaval whose ultimate consequences we might witness while Pluto passes through Libra, thus 90 degrees further in the zodiac. Pluto is now in Libra and will remain there until 1984, a year given special interest by the famous novel.

One may begin the geocentrically considered cycle of a planet's revolution around the Sun from the North Node of the planet, because the planetary nodes are the two ends of the intersection between the orbit of the planet and the orbit of the Earth. The North Node therefore begins the cycle of relationship between the two orbits; and, from the point of view of the heliocosm considered as a whole, a planet is represented by its orbit far more basically than by its physical mass—the latter indicating at any time the section of the orbital space being activated by the material globe. From such a point of view, and insofar as mankind is concerned, the beginning of an entire Pluto cycle (lasting about 248 years) occurred when Pluto reached for the first time its North Node during the fall 1929, almost exactly at the time of the stock market crash. It was "stationary retrograde" late in October; the crash occurred October 29th.

Pluto had been in Cancer approximately between 1665 and 1690. This was the time when Versailles, the court of the French monarch Louis XIV, was the focal point of European culture. It was also in Cancer during the early part of the fifteenth century, when Joan of Arc fought and was killed—a time which saw the beginning of the modern nation—and during the Crusades in the twelfth century, when the Gothic culture flourished and its great cathedrals were built. Earlier still its transit through Cancer marked the spread of Islam (seventh century), and during the first half of the first century B.C., the triumph of Rome—all important periods of sociocultural consolidation, but, in most instances, as the result of the destruction of governments or cultures whose time had come for disintegration.

When a generation is born with Pluto in Cancer, one can expect that some twenty to thirty years later individuals belonging to it and who are ready for personal transformation will have to deal with the consequences of what happened at the time of their birth. The generation born after 1913 was faced with World War II and the Cold War. It learned very little from the message of Pluto-in-Cancer in spite of all the pressures brought upon the old social system by the Jazz Age, the Boom, and the Depression, and the obvious trend toward technocratic and global patterns of organization.

Pluto in LEO (August 1938 to Spring-Summer 1957)

The entrance of Pluto in Leo brings us to the prelude to World War II, i.e., Nazi Germany's rearmament and invasion of Austria and Czechoslovakia. The collective glorification of the ego and the power-motive manifested in the rise of leaders only too ready to assume the responsibility of vast undertakings in war or peace, in government or in business. Huge organizations blossomed out and made use of the new technology. Atomic power revolutionized the relationship between nations. The Russian miracle transformed uneducated peasants into would-be cosmonauts, and a backward nation into one of two superpowers. New nations arose on the ruins of Europe's colonial hegemony: communist China, India, Israel, and many African nations. Modern psychology took a place of crucial prominence in our culture as the need to deal with the vagaries and crises of the personal ego became increasingly insistent.

Many of the inspirers of the youth protest of the sixties, and most of the hippies and their successors were born with Pluto in Leo. They are gradually becoming the leaders of a society in a state of increasing chaos, though the crucial decisions are still in the hands of the generation born with Pluto in Cancer, or even—especially at the level of the mind—in Gemini.

Pluto in Leo demands of us that we transmute our power-motive and our overemotional or overpossessive behavior. The biopsychic energy of life is being challenged, and when it fails to accept the challenge, death takes over. If men cannot unite in love, their blood must unite on the soil of battlefields stretching over the life-field of the Earth. It is not only the instinctive and superficial Martian aggressiveness that has to be sublimated, but a deeper craving for power, exteriorizing itself as pride and as a poignant sense of superiority which often hides under a feeling of inferiority.

Previous passages of Pluto through Leo occurred at the close of the seventeenth century, when the classical period of European culture was most brilliant, and when the modernization of Russia was beginning under Peter the Great. In the fifteenth century, the Catholic Medieval Order was nearing its end, with the slow rise of modern nations and the incipient Humanistic Movement. Constantinople fell to the Turks and the flight of Byzantine scholars to Italy was a catalyst to the eventual Renaissance. Long before this, Caesar came to power and was assassinated (44 B.C.), and some five centuries later, while Pluto was also crossing the sign Leo, Rome was destroyed by the Vandals, after having been saved a few years before by a bishop of Rome—named Leo.

Pluto in VIRGO (Summer 1957 to Autumn 1971)

Virgo is a symbol of the harvesting of karmic results. The emotional intensity, the self-glorification and power-hunger of the Leo type are now challenged, together with all the taken-for-granted traditions of the past. Everything is being criticized, often repudiated. Old relationships are broken up in the name of ideals often as yet imprecise. The high point of the last transit of Pluto through Virgo was the conjunction of Uranus and Pluto in 1965-66. The youth protest increased as the Vietnam War grew in importance; but its meaning was not understood, even by most young people.

Virgo is the technological sign par excellence, as it stresses the power of objective analysis and the reorganization of material units into new, yet impermanent combinations. Pluto in Virgo has referred to the computerization of our social processes, but also to retraining and reeducation, and to the search for new truths and new teachers or exemplars—thus the youth's fascination with Asiatic gurus.

The message of Pluto in Virgo is that the mind must be reoriented and repolarized so as to control the emotions and deal with the karma of the past, while visualizing as clearly as possible the outlines of the future. Some of the people born with Pluto in Virgo will mature at the time of the crisis expectable around 1989-90. Those born around 1965-66 should be in the forefront of whatever transformative activity takes place. Modern Freemasonry, which began in 1717 when Pluto was in Virgo, played a most important role in the political upheaval at the end of the century. Several of the Encyclopedists, Diderot, d'Alembert, Cadillac, and even Jean-Jacques Rousseau, apostle of a new type of education, were born with Pluto in Virgo. The Humanist Movement of the fifteenth century can also be identified with the same Pluto transit.

Pluto in LIBRA (Autumn 1971 to Winter 1984)

Pluto's transit in Libra, the zodiacal sign marking the fall equinox, is short because the planet's speed passes that of Neptune, but it may witness a series of important events which are basically related to changes that occurred while it was passing through the vernal equinox sign, Aries (1822-51). Then the Industrial Revolution had revealed its true colors and aroused strong reactions, including the birth in 1848 of World Communism with Marx and Engels' *Manifesto*. What we are facing today is the end result of the radical social, cultural, and political changes brought about by this Industrial Revolution. It can be related also to the period of World War I when Pluto passed through the summer solstice sign, Cancer.

Libra is the symbol of interrelatedness and of mutuality. Pluto in that sign tells us in no uncertain terms that new concepts of relationship must not only be imagined, but applied—and if need be, ruthlessly applied so that those who resist change may be permanently left out or "atomicized." Human beings who, under the transit through Cancer, could not be transformed as individuals within their home, community, or nation now are likely to experience a forced collective transformation. The present worldwide oil situation is a good example of how the pressure for change can work. The basic power for socioeconomic relationships is being curtailed. Human beings may be compelled to change their modes of association, and this naturally implies business changes and a deep reorganization of international relationships—and possibly wars and/or terrorism.

Libra may mean harmonization; but if obstacles stand in the way, they can be bulldozed efficiently once the Libra character is sufficiently aroused. In any case, in Libra we have the fateful reaction, or the wise response, to what occurred long ago. Both can be subtle, but effective. Theoretically, Pluto in Libra could affect the arts, but it may pulverize and atomicize what remains of old attitudes and traditions after Neptune (and before it

Uranus) has passed through the sign. The first atomic reaction occurred soon after the entry of Neptune in Libra; and the Watergate situation is a good instance of Pluto in Libra, especially as the U.S. birth chart (July 4, 1776 at 5:12 P.M.) has Libra on its Mid-Heaven. What we are witnessing may be only the start of a process which may last until Pluto returns to Aries around 2070: and that date is very close to what I consider to be the beginning of the Aquarian Age.[4]

Pluto in SCORPIO (1984 to Autumn 1995)

Pluto reaches its nearest point to the Sun (perihelion) in 1989 and all through Scorpio it moves within Neptune's theoretical orbit. Scorpio is a symbol of concentrated power which can have either highly positive healing and psychic vibrations, or negative ones, such as jealousy, vindictiveness, and secrecy—these being the results of a gnawing feeling of insecurity and frustration. Because this sign symbolizes an intense yearning for communion in depth with other human—or superhuman—beings (a yearning which is easily frustrated in view of our moralistic Christian tradition), it has usually been given a bad reputation; and so has Pluto. But what Pluto in Scorpio is likely to demand of us is that we truly and unhesitatingly plumb the depths of our common humanity. We may witness during that period a collective and compulsive kind of depth-psychology at work. This could take a religious form. We might be coerced into being truly "human" by contacts with beings of other planets or realms of existence, for we only come to learn what we are when faced by what definitely and unquestionably we are not—thus also by totally alien, non-earthly entities. This could be a time when human beings experience deeply and convincingly the feeling of "community" in a planet-wide sense. It could also witness the public and global operation of occult powers, both in individuals and in the field of social and political organization—perhaps through the appear-

4 Cf. Dane Rudhyar *Astrological Timing: The Transition to the New Age* (New York: Harper and Row, 1970, paperback edition).

ance of a powerful personage or avatar. When Pluto was last in Scorpio, men were born who became channels through which the deep transformative urge of Romanticism began to be felt. Others are now known as Fathers of American democracy (Thomas Paine, Thomas Jefferson, John Hancock, etc.).

Pluto in SAGITTARIUS (From approximately 1995 to 2010, and in the preceding cycle from 1750 to 1763-64)

In this zodiacal sign, Pluto is beginning to slow down and to transfer and interpret at a more mental but also more general and public level, the type of experiences which marked its transit through Scorpio. After the great emotional crisis which European man experienced in the year 1000 (the end of the world was then expected), when nothing catastrophic occurred, a deep upsurge of cultural activity and commercial travel took place with Pluto in Sagittarius. We might expect a similar type of development when the twentieth century ends, and about the time seven planets once more congregate in Taurus (2001). During the eighteenth century, the transit of Pluto through Sagittarius coincided with the war between England and France which started in America and spread to Europe. The defeat of France paved the way for the establishment of the U.S., but also for the eventual establishment of the British Empire, which was a foreshadowing of the future world-organization. Jean-Jacques Rousseau's book *The Social Contract*, published at the close of this period, was also an influential factor in both the American and the French revolutions.

Pluto in CAPRICORN (Approximately from 1764 to 1778)

Capricorn refers to the establishment of large-scale social schemes and political institutions, but also to their crystallization, which Pluto confronts and often radically upsets. The United States of America began its career under such a Pluto transit, which challenged the rights of the English king, particularly in matters of financial policy. Pluto is in the second House of the

U.S. chart with mid-Sagittarius rising, a highly significant position as the new nation found in the land of its birth tremendous resources which it ruthlessly and relentlessly tapped and indeed misused because of corporate greed and personal ambition.[5] In France, the monarchy was crumbling under a variety of scandals. Pluto often tends to bring into the open the shadow of political power or personal ambition. It forces any entrenched group to surrender its privilege or else to face revolution or moral-spiritual bankruptcy. It seems probable that Pluto had recently entered Capricorn when Luther challenged the powerfully entrenched Catholic Church.

Pluto in AQUARIUS (1778 to 1797-98)

Pluto's challenge was then directed to those who had upset the traditional order. As ideals had to be made concrete and workable, the revolutionists' triumph could be followed by harsh problems. A conservative U.S. Constitution followed an idealistic Declaration; and in France, Bonaparte dreamed of empire after the chaotic years of the Revolution. The basis of the Industrial Revolution was laid down by various technological inventions, especially the steam engine (Watts). The message of Pluto in Capricorn is that ideals have to be translated into some form of large-scale organization if they are to be effective. As Pluto moved through Aquarius in the sixteenth century, daring Europeans kept on with their exploration and conquest of South and North **America (Pizarro in Peru, Cartier in Canada).**

Pluto in PISCES (1798 to 1822-23)

This was the Napoleonic period in Europe and a time of stress in the new American nation. The use of steam engines in railroads—the locomotive (1814)—the discovery of electromagnetism

[5] The second House deals with what the incarnating Self is able to use at birth—its body and innate capacities—in order to build its individual personality. Cf. *The Astrological Houses.*

and its eventual use in telegraphy marked the spread of the Industrial Revolution which was to completely undermine the old European and American orders. Pisces can be the symbol of an inner war against the ghosts of the past. Napoleon sought to destroy the old national system of Europe, but he became possessed by a still older archetype, that of the Roman Empire. He failed his "star." The time had not come for Pluto to transform the consciousness of mankind as a whole. It only operated—except in rare cases—at the unconscious level of the planetary Mind, exerting pressure steadily wherever there was a receptive individual mind.

Pluto in ARIES (1823 to 1851-52)

Here Pluto was at work conveying to mankind, as much as man could receive, directives for a new world order. At first, unfortunately, the period witnessed a reaction against the Napoleonic dream, but in a more "modern" way the British Empire took its succession and the Victorian Age sanctified the power of the new class, the bourgeoisie—which in turn evoked the unavoidable response outlined in Marx and Engels' *Communist Manifesto.* A new religious movement that for the first time announced the coming of a world order—the movement started by the Bab in Persia (1844) and his thousands of martyred followers, and later transformed into the Baha'i faith—worked toward the union of human beings of all races and creeds. "Mankind" became not only a word, but a *potential* global reality. Modern science began to dominate the collective mentality of Western man on the basis of the practical application of postulates and universal laws formulated during the sixteenth and seventeenth centuries. What had started during the Renaissance with Pluto in Aries and Taurus came therefore to fruition a whole Pluto cycle afterward.

Pluto in TAURUS (1852 to 1883-84)

This was the period of scientific materialism symbolized by the Victorian Age and in France the days of the Second Empire which led to Germany's triumph. It was a time when power was worshipped on an unparalleled scale by nations and robber barons. Darwin, Marx, Pasteur, and a host of scientists-engineers set the patterns that provided the material framework for our modern Western society. The Romantic and Humanitarian Movements of the Pluto-in-Aries period became absorbed. Yet the spread of American spiritualism, of the Theosophical Society (started in New York in 1875), of Christian Science, and of various attempts at introducing Oriental philosophy to the West operated at counterpoint to the official trend of modern science.

Pluto in GEMINI (1884 to 1912-13)

What was substantiated and seemingly consolidated during the transit of Pluto through Taurus became not only further intellectualized, but also challenged, and brought to a state of transformative crisis, as Pluto moved through Gemini. This was the period when the spiritual-mental harvest of the European culture was reaped; but the harvest revealed a crucial need for a fundamental mutation, because it proved to be essentially tragic in that it fatefully led to World War I. Pluto in Gemini operated through the minds of men who were made acutely aware of the necessity for a radical transformation of the collective mentality of our Western world, and in non-Western countries of what was left of ancient concepts. The conjunctions of Neptune and Pluto in early Gemini (1891-92) brought to a focus this realization of a crucial need for renewal along trans-Saturnian and transpersonal lines. That twenty-seven-year period should thus be considered the "seed culmination" of the last Pluto cycle which had started in the mid-seventeenth century; yet at the same time it saw the birth of some men who were able to release intuitive visions of a future society.

These archetypal perceptions in many instances became temporarily submerged during the period between the two world wars (Pluto in Cancer), yet the ineluctable pressure of new worldwide developments led to the second and tragic phase of the Pluto cycle (Pluto in Leo) with its emphasis on personal power and imaginative technological inventions, particularly the use of atomic power. The third phase (Pluto in Virgo) revealed the triumph of Euro-American technology with its computers and flights to outer space; and we are now in the fourth phase (Pluto in Libra) which is bringing to mankind the imperative need for world-organization and for a radical transformation of all forms of interpersonal, intergroup, and international relationship. What we shall be able to achieve in meeting such a need will determine the kind of events with which mankind will be confronted during the fifth phase (Pluto in Scorpio)—the crucial, all-human period of testing. The individuals, groups, and nations which will have proved successful (i.e., *galactically oriented* in consciousness) shall progress further on the Path of service and discipleship during the sixth phase (Pluto in Sagittarius); the rest will disintegrate further or be absorbed as humus in a future rebirth of civilization.

Neptune in Zodiacal Signs

At this time of mankind's evolution, the cycle of Pluto provides the basic rhythm of the process of human transformation. One may speak in this case of deep oceanic currents, or better still perhaps of the tidal effect of gravitational forces external to our globe. When we consider Neptune's cycle of revolution through the tropical zodiac, we have to think of how this vast tidal motion manifests according to the specific shape of the shoreline of the continental regions. In some places the tides are hardly noticeable; in others, they are very strong and the water may move quite fast over the very gradually sloping ground. In such an illustration, Uranus' action would refer to the power of the wind which produces storms and high waves.

Neptune's North Node is now located at 11°32' of the sign Leo, but it has moved about half a degree since 1920, so that Neptune reached its North Node around October 1, 1919. It was stationary at 11°37' in mid-November, one year after the armistice concluding World War I was signed, and one year before the first meeting of the League of Nations in Geneva (November 15, 1920)—the first characteristically Neptunian type of global institution. The League of Nations was part of the peace treaty signed on June 28, 1919; but the U.S. Senate refused to ratify it—an action which made World War II inevitable and involved a heavy antigalactic karma for our country for having opposed the eventually inescapable Neptunian tide.

Neptune in LEO (From 1915 to 1928-29)

As Neptune's revolution around the tropical zodiac lasts about 164 years, this planet entered the sign Leo in 1751 and in 1587. It will reach that sign once more in 2079. It remains about thirteen and a half years in each sign. It is now, since 1970-71, in Sagittarius having accomplished one third of its zodiacal journey since it reached its North Node in 1919.

The period 1915-29 saw not only the end of the war and the peace that brought no peace, but the so-called Jazz Age whose ebullience and protests were partially sparked by the tragic blunder of prohibition, leading to the rise of organized crime. If Neptune is the Universal Solvent of Alchemy, this solvent became then bootleg and homemade alcohol. Above all, national leaders—except Woodrow Wilson—proved incapable of grasping the Neptunian spirit of internationalism and worldwide brotherhood. As a result, Neptune's power made "international Communism" the most effectual force, while the League of Nations floundered in uncertainty and confusion. It was also during that period that the great flu epidemic of 1918-19 killed millions of people.

Individuals born while Neptune passed through Leo came of age between 1936 and 1950. They were active during the great Depression and many died during World War II. Neptune sought to convey to them the message that their sense of self—their ego—had to lose its traditional rigidity and to become open to the archetype of what became popularly known between the two world wars as the Unconscious. Depth-psychology became fashionable; so did progressive education. Roosevelt's New Deal found in many youths an enthusiastic response, because it offered to them a new field for ego-expansion at the social level.

Neptune in VIRGO (1929 to 1942)

This was the depression period after the deceiving boom of the postwar years—and the start of World War II. Mankind had to pay for its refusal to listen to the message of Neptune in Leo. In Virgo, Neptune seeks to spiritualize the critical and analytical character of our modern intellect, but what could be an urge to the expansion of the mind along universalistic lines often turns out to be a fascination for big, yet unsound, dreams. The repressed forces of the collective Unconscious can irrupt into the unsteady and acquisitive ego-consciousness and spread destructively, as they did in a defeated Germany. Such a Neptunian transit occurred between 1765 and 1779; and at the constructive level we have the idealism of the Declaration of Independence. A previous transit began in 1601 at the close of Elizabeth's reign and as Galileo sought to publicize the heliocentric system.

Individuals born with Neptune in Virgo reached maturity in the fifties and sixties of this century, beginning the youth's protest against our rationalistic and technological society. They were the beatniks and the first of the psychedelic generation. They listened, entranced, to Neptune's voice, but often were not ready

to translate what they heard into the language of constructive
action (nor were they allowed to do so by the "silent majority"
and its revered Establishment).

Neptune in LIBRA (1942 to 1956-57)

   These were the war years for America, and the first and very
brief contact of Neptune with the 1st degree of Libra in December
1941 coincided with the first demonstration of a controlled atomic
chain reaction in Chicago. The United Nations organization was
formed, carrying a bit further the Neptunian ideal of a world-so-
ciety which the League of Nations had failed to actualize. The
idea of the "group" gradually spread among seekers after spiritual
realizations, and group psychology became increasingly accepted.
Many new nations were born. World trade and world finance
increasingly linked the continents, while television made it possible for human beings almost everywhere to experience and
sympathize with people of all races and cultures. Music also en-
joyed a great boom thanks to radio, tape recorders, and electronic
amplifiers. Earlier transits of Neptune in Libra occurred from
1779 to 1793 (the struggle to create an American Federal State—
and the breakdown of the French monarchy) and from 1616 to
1629-30 (Francis Bacon, *Novum Organum,* crystallizing the Nep-
tune-in-Virgo influence).
   Individuals born with Neptune in Libra are now reaching or
have reached maturity. They constitute the postwar generation
faced by the task of developing new forms of interpersonal, social,
and political relationships under the influence of Neptune. Most
of them have had experiences with drugs in a society dominated
by chemicals and psychological problems. Will they be able to
respond constructively and fearlessly to the universalistic, non-
possessive, and nonaggressive power which the Galaxy has been
focusing through Neptune during their youth, or will they merely
react confusedly to the Neptunian acid that always seeks to dis-

solve what had refused to accept change, and positively work at a wholesome transition to a new age?

Neptune in SCORPIO (1957 to 1970)

This was a very disturbed period because Scorpio refers to the urge within individuals to experience total fusion or blending with another individual, or a very intimate participation in a cohesive and more or less ritualistic group—big business being the modern way of ritualistic living in a profit-mad society. When Neptunian energies act upon such an urge, they tend to over glorify the experiences of communion by giving them cosmic or mystical overtones—even if it is only the mystique of power and money. Few people can bear the transcendent and totally unfamiliar character of these experiences and therefore either become psychically lost in their results, or else they materialize and degrade the experiences, which leads to lust, sadism, black magic, and all forms of violence.

When the individuals born under such a Neptune transit will be confronted by the presence of Pluto in Scorpio—they may be then in their late twenties or in their teens—the results of their early experiences are likely to take a definite and ineluctable form, for better or for worse. They and the Neptune-in-Libra generation may well then decide which turn our society will take, or their own personal fate.

Neptune entered Scorpio in November 1792 (the Terror during the French Revolution) and left the sign in 1806 after Napoleon had proclaimed himself "Emperor of the French." The previous transit had lasted from 1629 to 1643, and can be related to the growing conflict between Catholics and Protestants.

Neptune in SAGITTARIUS (1970 to 1984)

Babies are now born with Neptune in this sign referring to all kinds of expansive activities, physical or metaphysical. Mental processes which seek to understand the principles and patterns of organization structuring whatever the mind contemplates can be referred to Sagittarius. What began while Neptune was transiting Leo, especially since 1919, might reach a higher level of effectiveness; and this new generation may be able to actualize some of the ideals which seeped through the World War I ruins of the old European culture. The boys and girls now being born will reach their youthful maturity at the beginning of the next century. Those who will have *significantly* survived the last two decades of this century may have a real chance of proving themselves architects of a new society: the actual building processes may have to wait until Neptune reaches Capricorn. Neptune's message now is that mankind should not remain at the Jupiterian level of political and managerial ambition and greed for power. The children now coming to this world should be shown that only all-encompassing principles—social, ethical, cultural, or political —can be worth fighting for. While Jupiter excludes the alien, Neptune accepts, evaluates, and finds a place for each of the most disparate elements.

Neptune was in Sagittarius from 1806-07 to 1820-21. The Napoleonic dream was shattered and in the process England and the U.S. fought an inconclusive war. At the same time South American nations were born, which may have a great future at the close of this century. Mexico and Brazil gained their independence as Neptune entered Capricorn in conjunction with Uranus. A cycle before, Neptune entered Sagittarius in 1643, leaving the sign in 1656-57. This was the Cromwellian period and the triumph of the Puritans. The rationalistic spirit of the classical period was triumphing, yet countercultural forces were also at work. However, man was not yet aware of Neptune's existence and the time had not come for a public realization of the nature of the planet's galactic message to mankind.

Neptune in CAPRICORN (1984 to 1998)

During such a transit Neptune participates in a massing of many planets in this zodiacal sign. After 1988 Saturn and Uranus will join Neptune, with Mars part of the time in Capricorn (1988 and 1990). In 1990 Jupiter opposes the group, and Venus and Mercury add their weight to the Capricorn group during January-February. This could be a highly disturbing period, perhaps involving telluric changes, as well as heavy political pressures. It might also see a forceful attempt at building a global state or the spread of an authoritarian world-religion. Pluto's transit through Scorpio, in sextile to the Capricorn stellium of planets, may turn out to be the dominant factor during that period.

Neptune was in Capricorn as Louis XIV autocratically ruled France and during the triumph of the classical spirit. In England the great London fire occurred and the restoration of the monarchy took place after Oliver Cromwell's death (1658). Neptune reached Capricorn in conjunction with Uranus in 1820-21 and left the sign in 1834. Reactionary forces dominated Europe. The first railroads were built. But in 1830 an emergent revolutionary spirit placed the bourgeois king Louis Philippe I on the throne of France and other political revolutions followed, eventually leading to more radical changes in 1848.

Neptune in AQUARIUS (1834 to 1848; and after 1998)

Neptune in Aquarius reached its South Node at the time it was discovered in 1846. From then on, its ability to focus upon the human masses the aspect of galactic power to which it is attuned becomes more obvious. Its discovery corresponds to the early beginning of several movements already mentioned, all of which aim at uniting large collectivities all over the world and—ideally,

at least—the whole of mankind. Thus, what occurred in the nineteenth century evokes the strong possibility that a similar kind of
global activity may transform mankind from 1998 to about
2011-12 when the planet once more reaches Aquarius. In May
2000 all the heliocosmic planets, plus the Sun and the Moon—
seven planets altogether—are focusing their power in Taurus,
squared by Uranus and Neptune in Aquarius; an interesting
beginning for the twenty-first century!

Neptune in PISCES (1848 to 1862)

In Pisces, Neptune is in the zodiacal sign in which it is most
effective, and we see Neptunian forces at work dissolving the
structures of the past. This is the Romantic Age, and that of the
triumph of the bourgeoisie of wealth and the higher middle class.
The long-ruling Austrian emperor, Francis-Joseph I, came to the
throne in 1848 and his reign, ending in 1916, marked the progressive disintegration of Central Europe and of the old imperial
concept inherited from the Rome of the Caesars. This was the
Victorian era in England and the ill-fated Second Empire in
France; while in America, the U.S. increased enormously in size
after the war with Mexico, and the Gold Rush led men westward.
Japan was forced to open her harbor to foreign commerce; the
rise of this new Asiatic power had great consequences, ending
with Pearl Harbor a century later.

Neptune in ARIES (1861 to 1875)

This was the period of Germany's rise, with Bismarck as its
architect. Italy also became unified and the Papacy was shorn of
its power. The American Civil War began in April 1861 just as
Neptune entered Aries for a few months, then regressed to Pisces
until February 1862. A new nation actually took form under the
pressure of industrial expansion and the destruction of the cul-

ture of the South. While Saturn refers to relatively narrow and local principles of organization, Neptune symbolizes more encompassing—thus "Federal" rather than "State"—structures. The stage was set for the growth of large nations with worldwide interests and ambitions, and colonialism. But among men born with Neptune in Aries, we find Lenin, Sri Aurobindo (one of the first Indians to fight for his country's independence), and Gandhi.

Neptune in TAURUS (1874-75 to 1888)

Colonialism now dominated the world-stage, Africa being almost totally divided between European nations. Neptune participated in a massive constellation of six and even seven planets in this zodiacal sign of productivity and materialism (1881-82). President Franklin D. Roosevelt and a number of statesmen and philosophers who became famous some fifty years later were born during that period. So were the psychologist Carl Jung and Pope John XXIII.

Neptune in GEMINI (1888-89 to 1901-02)

The most important astrological event of that period was the conjunction of Neptune and Pluto in 1891-92. This marked the beginning of a five-hundred year cycle and of the great revolution in science which was soon to upset most of the basic concepts taken for granted by the nineteenth-century mentality. Backed by the as-yet undiscovered Pluto, Neptune conveyed to mankind new cosmic *information* that made the old intellectual categories obsolete. As the twentieth century began, Neptune and Pluto in Gemini were opposing all other planets—seven of them (including Sun and Moon) being gathered in Sagittarius at the New Moon (solar eclipse) preceding January 1, 1900, when the new century (characterized by the digits 19) began. Quantum physics and Freudian depth-psychology opened wide the doors to the mental upheaval. At the same time, the U.S. was embarking on an expansionistic international policy, which Theodore Roosevelt was to implement with typical vigor when he became President—thus laying the foundations for the display of world-power soon to be demonstrated by our country.

Neptune in CANCER (1902 to 1913-15)

This period, which has been referred to as *La Grande Epoque,* saw the swan song of the old European culture and the harsh sounds of political conflicts and ultimately of the German army's advance into Belgium and France, ushering World War I. In 1914 Neptune was entering Leo just after Pluto had settled in Cancer together with Saturn. The preceding challenge in Gemini to the collective mentality of Western Man was now directed toward his proud ego (Leo) and its foundation, the patriarchal home, and its traditional way of life (Cancer).

Many of today's leaders were born with Neptune in Cancer, a few with Neptune in Gemini. As we already saw, Neptune reached its North Node in 1919-20 on the 12th degree of Leo, where Jupiter joined it at the time of President Wilson's unsuccessful attempt to have the Senate ratify the peace treaty and thus allow the United States to participate in the League of Nations. This Wilsonian failure led to the tragic tensions and passionate protests connected with the transit of Neptune through Scorpio, forty years later and 90 zodiacal degrees further—especially the Vietnam quagmire, a long-delayed karmic result of the American isolationism, and of the fear of Soviet Russia which has marked America's policy since the Twenties.

Uranus in Zodiacal Signs

Uranus takes on an average 83.75 years to circle the tropical zodiac and remains seven years in each sign. Its North Node was at

13°51′ Gemini in 1973, progressing apparently at the rate of 18 seconds per year. It should therefore now be located on the fifteenth degree of Gemini. The heliocentric passage of the planet Uranus over its (also heliocentric) North Node occurred on July 20th, 1945, four days after the first atomic explosion in Alamagordo, New Mexico. The previous passage had occurred in June 1861, just after Lincoln's inauguration and the start of the Civil War. Other crossings occurred in 1777 during the War of Independence, and in 1693, 1609, and 1526.

It seems difficult to pin down in general terms the messages of Uranus to mankind and especially to individuals, because they are conditioned by particular needs, depending on the way Saturn has been operating. Uranus' purpose is to break down the continuity of Saturnian patterns, so that at the place and time of the break some kind of galactically oriented vision, or intuitive flash of thought, may be experienced.

Generally speaking, during the passage of Uranus through a zodiacal sign, the non-normal and transcendental aspects of the mode of activity which the sign usually represents are allowed to operate wherever the Saturnian sociocultural ways of life and personal habits have lost some of their prestige and unquestioned validity. But it is not easy to formulate what these "non-normal and transcendental aspects" are. What is essential is that the normal, traditional, and matter-of-fact patterns of behaving, feeling, and thinking should have led to suffering, frustration, defeat, and tragedy, or even acute boredom and a sense of total futility. When this occurs, Uranus is always ready to act, and it acts more specifically in terms of the possibilities inherent in the type of energy characterizing the zodiacal sign in which Uranus is then located. The Uranian process is also polarized by what planetary aspects at the time allow to happen; and it usually deals with experiences related to the House of the natal chart which the planet is crossing by transit.

If one seeks to understand the position of Uranus in a birth chart—that of a collective as well as an individual person—it is logical to expect that this zodiacal position is in some manner related to the person's karma, or to some *inertial tendency* karmically inherent in the person's nature. Uranus acts where, in some ancient past, there had been bondage and compulsive behavior. When Saturn and Uranus are in the same sign a particularly strong karmic pressure is likely to be felt by the individuals born at that time. The mean period between the conjunctions of these two planets is about forty-five years. They were conjunct in Libra in 1805 (the Napoleonic challenge to old aristocratic ways in Europe), in Taurus in 1852, in Scorpio (three times) in 1897, and in Taurus in 1942. They will be conjunct three times in Sagittarius during 1988, a time which may see some outstanding religious and social upheaval, and may particularly affect the United States, whose birth chart has a Sagittarian Ascendant (July 4, 1776, 5:12 P.M., Philadelphia).[6] These last mentioned conjunctions occur in the last degrees of Sagittarius close to the point at which the center of the Galaxy is reflected upon our tropical zodiac. Following this, Saturn and Uranus will join Neptune in Capricorn, with Jupiter opposing them from Cancer, a sign also strongly emphasized in the U.S. chart by the presence of the Sun, Venus, Jupiter, and Mercury in Cancer.

In the twentieth-century chart (midnight January 1, 1900) and in that for the preceding New Moon, which is important in a study of the vital forces at work throughout the century, Uranus and Saturn are both in Sagittarius, surrounded by many planets and broadly opposed by Neptune and Pluto in Gemini—a remarkable symbol of the basic ideological and sociopolitical conflicts characterizing our century. The Uranian challenge is focused on all that Sagittarius represents in the religious, social, and philosophical spheres. It was the time when Planck's quantum theory upset the foundations of physics, and Freud did the same in the field of psychology. The Victorian era ended in 1901. The Dreyfus affair disrupted the unity of the French peo-

6 Cf. *The Astrology of America's Destiny* (New York: Random House, 1974).

ple, challenging the integrity of the judicial and military systems and opening a period of conflict between the State and the Church. Germany began to build a powerful Navy, thus challenging the foundations of England's power. The Spanish-American War started, at least partially stirred up by William Randolph Hearst and his newspapers catering to sensationalism, as Uranus (with Saturn close by) was entering Sagittarius. Uranus was at Sagittarius 13°6′ on the degree of the Ascendant of the U.S. chart when President McKinley was shot on September 14, 1901—one of many justifications for this rising degree. Theodore Roosevelt's powerful and aggressive administration began a new phase in the development of the collective consciousness of the American people.

When Uranus entered Capricorn in 1905 the Panama Canal was purchased and the Russo-Japanese War had just begun, which drew America's attention toward the Pacific and led to President Roosevelt's mediation role at the peace table, a role which deeply angered the Japanese. The great San Francisco earthquake and fire occurred in 1906. New forces began to play in the artistic world bringing a challenge to traditional styles and institutions (Cubism with Picasso, the orientalistic influence of Diaghilev's Russian Ballets, etc.). A considerable ferment operated throughout Europe underneath a glowing façade of prestigious culture. Germany was increasing her challenges to England and France. The abortive 1905 revolution in Russia heralded the future upheaval.

The entrance of Uranus into Aquarius during the winter of 1912 marked the beginning of the process which let to World War I. The first Balkan War began in the fall of 1912, having been preceded by a war between Italy and Turkey. The summer of 1914 saw the beginning of World War I, as Saturn was moving through the seventh House (the Allies) of the U.S. chart. If Aquarius is the sign of "reforms," the passage of Uranus through it during the entire war suggests how a Uranus transit may operate. The war represented a special type of approach to the reform of mankind, especially in the Western world. The Bolshevik Revolution occurred in November 1917. Individuals born during the war carry therefore the astrological signature of Uranus in Aquarius. After coming of age they had to face the challenge of World War II.

Uranus was in Pisces between 1919-20 and the spring of 1927; this period saw the Jazz Age, the Prohibition era, the financial boom. In Germany and Central Europe these were tragic years. Soviet Russia struggled in the midst of radical social reforms and famine, and suffered the hostility of the capitalistic "Allies." Many American intellectuals emigrated to Western Europe, where Dadaism, Surrealism, and German Expressionism captivated an inttelligentsia tragically aware of cultural disintegration and of the end of a cycle (Pisces).

The coming of Uranus to Aries in 1927 did not improve matters, at least outwardly. It led, first in Europe, then in the U.S., to the great Depression. But Uranus was still in Aries when Franklin D. Roosevelt came to power and stemmed the debacle of capitalism, for which the wealthy (strangely enough) came to hate him. Nevertheless he transformed the U.S. government and, through a strong income tax, many of the ways of American life. The power of American universities and of educational or religious foundations, most often managed by professors or powerful business men, brought a deep-seated change in the cultural life of America—a change whose character and scope is not sufficiently appreciated, and its value assessed. Technology and the transformation of all concepts related to management made rapid progress.

The period outlined by the passage of Uranus through Taurus (1935–1942) constituted the prelude to World War II and the rise of Mussolini, Hitler, and the Japanese military. The Western world struggled to emerge from the Depresssion and unemployment, and Taurean problems of productivity occupied much of humanity's attention. The war actually began with Italy's aggression against Ethiopia, the Spanish Civil War, and Japan's invasion of China in 1936. The uranium atom was split in 1939, and the first controlled atomic reaction occurred on December 2, 1942 after Uranus had reached Gemini in June of that year. Pearl Harbor (Dec. 7, 1941) occurred as Uranus, still in Taurus, had reached the star Alcyone in the Pleiades, a star which ancient star-lore believed to be the center around which our solar system revolves—perhaps now an obsolete center for a humanity having reached a global awareness of all its component parts through the crucible of global tragedy!

The Gemini transit lasted until the summer of 1949. We have already seen that Uranus reached its North Node at the time of the first atomic bomb explosion. After that date the possibility of using atomic power dominates the world-stage, together with the remarkable rise of Soviet Russia as a great world power able to challenge the United States. The protesting youth of the sixties, not only in America but all over the world, was born with Uranus in Taurus and Gemini; some of their older inspirers having responded to the transforming challenge of Uranus in Aries (1927–35). Uranus in spring zodiacal signs tends to generate a restlessness eager for action.

As a new generation, born with Uranus in Cancer (from 1949 to 1955-56), comes to maturity, the urge to transform the deepest patterns of ego-consciousness and to develop an awareness beyond the range of the ego-controlled mind is gaining more and more momentum; thus the fascination exerted by Asiatic techniques like yoga, Zen, and Tibetan meditation—and also by all forms of parapsychology, psychic healing, clairvoyance, and astral travel.

Uranus was in Leo until 1962, and present-day teen-agers had such a configuration at birth. Many of them will presumably be important leaders at the time of the worldwide crisis anticipated just before and after 1990, when they will begin their dynamic twenties. The children born with the massive conjunctions of planets in Aquarius during February 1962 still had Uranus retrograde in Leo, conjunct the regal star, Regulus. They may play a particularly significant role. So also the younger ones born at the time of the conjunction of Uranus and Pluto in Virgo in 1965-66

—a very intense period in which to be born! They will be twenty-five in 1990, thirty-five when the new century begins. Yet the basic impulse may be given by individuals born as Uranus crossed Taurus and Gemini.

As we deal with the slow-moving, trans-Saturnian planets in individuals' charts, we should most specifically pay attention to their positions in the natal Houses, then to the time when they cross the four Angles and the Sun and the Moon of the natal chart. The transit of Uranus over the natal Sun of a person, in nearly all cases, indicates quite a basic change in his or her life pattern and/or consciousness, though such a change evidently can take an immense variety of forms. Some of these are clearly positive and inspiring; others at first will seem negative if they bring challenges which at least appear premature and too difficult for the individual to meet. In other instances it is the transit over the Ascendant or the Moon which focuses the most basic opportunity for life transformation.

The Houses in which Uranus, Neptune, and Pluto are located indicate the *category of experiences* which are most susceptible to become channels for the transformation of the Saturn-controlled and Sun-fascinated personality into an open vase able to absorb galactic values and inspiration. Everything in a birth chart tells us what is best for us. It reveals what are the optimal conditions for using the functions symbolized by the planets (always including the Sun and the Moon) in the performance of our dharma— our "truth-of-being" and our destiny. Such a performance might result in what we normally consider as tensions, harsh confrontations, illnesses, or the loss of what we had emotionally valued; but the human way, when illumined however faintly by the spiritual light of galactic consciousness, is one that requires of those who *consciously* tread it the courage and the readiness to learn how to absorb and assimilate, then transmute and transfigure, suffering and tragedy. It is the way of incarnation of the divine Idea in the resistant and dark materials, the remains of the unfinished business of past cycles.[7]

[7] For a study of the general meaning of Uranus, Neptune, and Pluto in natal Houses, see *The Astrological Houses*.

.6.

The Interpenetrating Cycles
of Uranus, Neptune, and Pluto

The fact that the periods of revolution around the Sun of the three trans-Saturnian planets are related in the simplest arithmetical way is highly significant. The Neptune period is twice—and the Pluto period three times—that of Uranus. Uranus therefore represents the basic unit in the already mentioned three-pronged challenge to the Saturn-Jupiter and the Mars-Venus-Mercury combinations. What Uranus begins, Neptune complements and extends, and Pluto finalizes the process. In most systems of symbolization, a thrice-repeated operation (or experience) is said to have reached a condition of irrevocability. It is so at least at the archetypal level; but when a material system opposes a strong inertial resistance to change, this three-beat rhythm may have to be repeated for a long time before its purpose is concretely achieved.[1]

---

[1] If one might interject here a note of whimsy, the process can be seen as similar to an old-fashioned waltz. After rapidly whirling around a sufficient number of times, the dizzy man and woman completely fall into each others arms and accomplish what they were intended to do from the beginning of the cosmic dance.

From the galactic point of view presented in this book, the basic fact is that we are dealing with one vast process of transformation; and one should be able to time its development by studying the interrelations linking the cycles of the three planets. There are years during which the three planets are in conjunction, or at least near-conjunction, although the exact years during which such a triple conjunction occurs are still uncertain, because the pattern of Pluto's revolutions is not precisely determined, and trans-Plutonian influences are likely at work over long periods. It seems fairly certain, however, that during the springs of 576 and 575 B.C., Uranus, Neptune, and Pluto were very close to conjunction in mid-Taurus. In 1082 B.C. they were apparently all three in Aries—but a number of degrees apart. A triple conjunction or near-conjunction may have occurred in 4517 B.C. and could be expected to recur around A.D. 2800. It is to be hoped that a truly reliable picture of the threefold cyclic interractions of these planets will soon be available, but this requires the accurate programming of computers, and the formulas which have been used seem to vary slightly. If definitive data were obtainable, we could gain a more objective overview of the development of mankind, especially during the brief period of five thousand years with which most of the study of history deals today.

It may be well to mention here that what is called "history," especially in the quasi-mystical sense which some philosophers last century gave to the word, refers only to the present-day consciousness of Western man as he seeks to bring into some sort of ordered, and to him significant, sequence the racial memory embodied in its particular culture. History deals with the collective subjectivity of a culture, or even of a special community or religious group. It embodies not merely so-called facts and records, but their interpretation. In ancient cultures, history had an essentially archetypal character, as it dealt primarily with transphysical and transfactual processes, for instance, the great *yugas* and *mahayugas* of Indian philosophers-seers. Today in our materialistically oriented Euro-American culture, history has mainly become a scholarly search for and "critcal" interpretation of physical records of so-called facts. But what exactly is a "fact"? Is it not only what most people agree to accept as such, very often in the ignorance of unseen or unacknowledged forces or operators which are the real actors?

Astronomical cycles should help us to understand not only the vast tidal rhythms of man's evolution underneath all the different waves accompanying the forming, culminating, and disintegrating local cultures, but the place which our present period occupies in the planetary tide of the development of human consciousness. The start of the particular phase of human development which today seems to have reached a crucial turning point can be traced to the triple conjunction of Uranus, Neptune, and Pluto during the sixth century B.C.[2] This was the century during which Gautama, the Buddha, Pythagoras, Zoroaster (the last of a series of prophets by the same name—according to the esoteric doctrines of the Parsis), Lao-Tze, and other great personages lived and taught. It marked the concrete beginnings of our Western civilization, even if one might speak of earlier roots related to the theism of the Bhagavat Gita, and to Chaldean, Egyptian, and Mosaic prenatal influences.

The Neptune-Pluto Cycle

In the course of some twenty-five centuries, there have been several conjunctions of Neptune and Pluto: during the spring of 82 B.C. (with Uranus then entering Aries, and with Jupiter and Saturn being conjunct in 84 B.C. in square to Neptune and Pluto); in A.D. 410; in 903; in 1397—apparently the first conjunction in Gemini; and in 1891-92. This means that five such Neptune-Pluto cycles have occurred between 576 B.C. and A.D. 1891, and that we

---

[2] In *The Secret Doctrine* (Theosophical Publishing House) H. P. Blavatsky mentions, without explanation, the year 607 B.C. as being "the end of the Archaic Ages."

are now in the sixth. According to their esoteric character, these numbers are quite revealing.

The period 576 to 82 B.C. has the Number 1 characteristic of a new beginning. It was unfortunately a beginning fatefully haunted and distorted by the ghosts of the past, yet at the same time reacting intellectually against this past and unable to realize how the new creative impulse was related to the spiritual harvest out of which it had emerged. This was the tragedy of the Athenian culture, still based on slavery while dreaming of democracy and trying to integrate the experiences of the Eleusinian and Orphic Mysteries with the new skepticism of Socrates and the intellectualism of the Sophists.

The second period witnesed the development and power of the Roman Empire, which left ineradicable marks upon European civilization. What had been the Greek ideal (No. 1) took the form of the Roman citizen (No. 2). The concept of "legal person" (collective as well as individual) found its spiritual correlate in Jesus' ideal of every man being a "Son of God" and thus endowed with an immanent spark of divinity—the God-seed within.

The third period saw the triumph of Christianity and the decay of imperial Rome (Alaric destroyed Rome in A.D. 410 about the time of the Neptune-Pluto conjunction). When phases 1 and 2 contain too much of unredeemable darkness, Number 3 turns destructive and produces the chaos from which the roots of a new attempt can draw sustenance; but this new attempt has to operate through a heavy cloud distorting the original sources of the culture. Islam, a response to the relative spiritual failure of Christianity, conquered most of the southern countries once dominated by the Roman Empire. The Papacy acquired political power, and this led to a second area of conflict during the Number 4 period, from A.D. 903 to 1397. This was the period of the Crusades, and of the great Medieval European Order dominated by a powerful Church fighting against ambitious Holy Emperors as well as against Near Eastern ideas introduced by the Arabs.

The fifth period began with the Humanist Movement, the

Renaissance, and the colonization of the Americas. It saw the triumph of rationalism, empiricism, mechanism, and materialism. No. 5 is the symbol of mind, but when the mind develops on the foundation of a formalistic, personalistic, and rigid approach to spirituality it is compelled to become equally dogmatic in its attempts to deal with whatever the still powerful religious heritage had downgraded and left uncultivated. It therefore becomes the empirical and rationalistic mind, so intent on dealing solely with the material world that it becomes moulded by the rhythms of matter.

The sixth period began in 1891-92 with the discovery of X-rays, radioactivity, the quantum, and Einstein's famous formula reducing matter to energy, and making of light the soul of space. As the twentieth century opened, an opposition of Uranus (and all other planets) to the conjunction of Neptune and Pluto symbolically announced an era of ideological conflicts as well as of brutal and global wars—the "Civil War of Man." We are now at the start of the last quarter of the century and the relationship of Neptune to Pluto is about to assume a very special character.

Because of the very elongated shape of Pluto's orbit, during a few years in each revolution of the planet around the Sun it comes closer to the Sun—and as well to the Earth—than Neptune ever does. As this occurs we can say, at least symbolically, that Pluto penetrates Neptune's orbit. I have interpreted this penetration as a kind of interplanetary process of "fecundation." This occurs about every 248 years and (according to the Naval Observatory in Washington, D.C.) it will take place between 1978 and 2000. Pluto will be at the point in its orbit closest to the Sun (perihelion) in 1989, presumably at Scorpio 13°.

These periods of fecundation of Neptune's orbit by Pluto have proved very significant in European history. They marked rather crucial, long-term events in the mid-eighteenth century, at the time of the "discovery" of America by Columbus and the Renaissance (1481–1503), during the great period of the Gothic cathedrals and the struggle between popes and emperors; at the critical time of the year 1000 which Europe expected to be the end of the world; during the apex of Arabic culture in the eighth century and the reign of Charlemagne which established the root-pattern of the European cycle; around the time of Clovis' conversion to Christianity, which marked the acceptance of the new religion by the main leader of the Germanic tribes; in the late third century; and presumably during Christ's ministry and the early growth of the churches under Paul.

Since Pluto, at the time it nears its perihelion in Scorpio, moves a little faster than Neptune, the aspect made by the two planets before their orbital interpenetration tends to be many times repeated. One can say that it lasts—"within orb"—as long as about ninety years. When Neptune entered Libra in October, 1942 (first sustained atomic reaction in Chicago, December 1942), Pluto was at Leo 7°—thus the two planets formed a broad sextile aspect (60°). If we give an 8-degree orb (maximum distance) to that aspect, it will last continuously until about the year 2038 when Pluto will reach the 17th degree of Aquarius and Neptune the 24th degree or Aries—thus, during a ninety-six-year period. During that time, there will be several years which will witness repeated exact sextiles of the two planets.

If, in order to simplify the picture, we consider the *heliocentric* positions of the planets, the first exact sextile occurred around January 1952 (from Leo to Libra 20°) and was repeated until January 1955; then Neptune forged a little ahead until 1979, when other exact sextiles will occur. After 1984, Pluto entering Scorpio begins to move definitely faster than Neptune entering Capricorn. The two planets will be about 68 degrees apart in 1997; but Pluto then begins to slow down a little and Neptune gradually moves ahead. In about 2065 Pluto in late Pisces should square Neptune in late Gemini. This is approximately the time which I have given for the start of the precessional Age of Aquarius—A.D. 2062.[3]

[3] Cf. *An Astrological Timing: The Transition to the New Age,* Chaps. 7–9.

The beginning of the "long sextile" between Neptune and Pluto during which we are now living, occurred some fifty years after the last conjunction of the two planets in 1891–92. It occurred also after the conjunction of 1397-98 and lasted from about 1450 to 1540. This was the period of the Renaissance, the Elizabethan Age, and in 1517 Luther's Reformation. The two planets had formed a semisquare aspect during the Hundred Years' War and the burning of Joan of Arc. They reached their "waxing" square around 1571-73 (wars of religion), their trine (120° aspect) at the close of the sixteenth century (the revocation of Nantes Edict which brought a small degree of religious tolerance). The opposition occurred in 1645—the Cromwellian era and the start of the classical period in France during the reign of Louis XIV. Neptune was at Sagittarius 5°, Pluto at Gemini 5°.

During the new Pluto period of some 248 years duration which followed—thus, until the Neptune-Pluto conjunction of 1891-92 —a long aspect occurred when Pluto came near its perigee around 1740-41. As Neptune was then in Cancer, the long aspect was a *trine*. It lasted from about 1698 to 1798—ending at the time of the adoption of the U.S. Constitution. Such a "long trine" occurred also during the last Crusades which had begun before an opposition of Neptune and Pluto. This was a great turning point in European history, as it brought the nobility of Western Europe in contact with Near-Eastern traditions and particularly with the Sufi influence. A "long trine" follows the opposition of Neptune and Pluto, while a "long sextile" (60° aspect) occurs some fifty or more years after their conjunction. However, as the conjunctions of the two planets move ahead in the zodiac, cycle after cycle, but Pluto's perigee presumably remains almost stationary, the character of the "long aspect" will change. The long sextile will be replaced by a long septile (51½°) and long semisquare (45°). The nature of the long aspect is determined by the length of the period separating the conjunction from the time Pluto begins to move almost as fast as Neptune and, a few years later, reaches its perigee. It seems that of late each conjunction has occurred about 5 degrees ahead of the preceding one; but this probably is not a constant value.

The Uranus-Pluto Cycle

Conjunctions of Uranus and Pluto have been said to take place every 127 years; but a thrice-repeated conjunction occurred in 1850 and late April 1851 on the last degrees of Aries—with Mercury, then Saturn in May 1851, and Mars and Venus a few days later, joining the pair—and the last conjunction (also thrice-repeated) took place on October 9, 1965 (18th degree of Virgo), and on April 4th, and June 30th, 1966 (17th degree). The interval between the two sets of conjunctions was therefore 115 years. Saturn played an important role in these conjunctions; it was conjunct to Uranus and Pluto in 1851 and opposed to it in 1965–66. Jupiter squared this opposition in May 1965 and remained squaring it, but less precisely, in March 1966. Mars was also involved, being in Virgo in 1965 and in Pisces in 1966.

In my recent book *The Astrology of America's Destiny* I stressed (pp. 119-127) the importance of the 1965-66 period, for this also was the time of the last "progressed New Moon" calculated from the U.S. birth chart for July 4, 1776. Progressed New Moon occurs at about thirty-year intervals; thus for the U.S. in 1787, 1816, 1846, 1876, 1905, 1935, and 1965. They produced a rhythmic pattern of growth in the *collective person*, which the United States, its people, and its land, constitute. As the progressed Lunation Cycle (from a progressed New Moon to the next) lasts thirty years, and as the last tenth of every cycle constitutes always a period of transition (or "seed period") leading to the next cycle, the three years from 1962 to 1965 have had a particular importance. They were marked by our progressive involvement in the undeclared Vietnam War, the confrontation with the Russians in Cuba, and the election and assassination of President Kennedy. During these years LSD became more widely known and used, especially by young people. The college youth's rebellion against the way in which universities were run began at the University of California in Berkeley during December 1964. It soon spread throughout the world. The revolt against the draft followed. The year 1965 witnessed also the Civil Rights Movement and the Watts riots in Los Angeles.

Martin Luther King and Robert Kennedy were assassinated in 1968 under rather suspicious circumstances somehow linking the murders—at least in many people's minds—to the assassination of President Kennedy.

The 1850-51 period was probably not as crucial for our country as 1965-66. In 1851 Cuba was declared independent; and Napoleon III's *coup d'état* started the ill-fated Second Empire in France which had drastic repercussions in Mexico, and eventually led to the formation of the German empire. The process of industrialization became more strongly set than ever, and it resulted in the spread of colonialization. The first submarine telegraphic cable was laid between England and France in 1851, an appropriate symbol of electric communication soon to link all continents. In our country in 1850, the Henry Clay Compromise made history, and California became the thirty-first state of a Union soon to be radically challenged by the Civil War.

The opposition between Uranus and Pluto was of great historical importance when it occurred in 1901 and 1902. These years marked the close of the long reign of Queen Victoria, the end of the South African War, the foundation of the Commonwealth of Australia, the beginning of acute conflicts between colonial powers and of Germany's colonial ambitions in Africa—one of the two or three main causes of World War I. In the Far East, the Boxer rebellion in China and the invasion of Manchuria by Russia led to the Russo-Japanese War, the rise of Japan, and indirectly to World War II in the Pacific. In America, the assassination of President McKinley on September 6, 1901, preceded by about three months the opposition of Uranus to Pluto; but as Uranus was crossing the U.S. natal Ascendant (the 14th degree of Sagittarius), the aggressive new President soon brought to a focus the international ambitions of our nation in a variety of Uranian actions.

Thus what had begun around the time of the Uranus-Pluto conjunction was becoming fulfilled at the time of the opposition. Industrial power and the ambition of modern nations backed by military force were becoming decisive factors in an international pattern of conflicts which could only lead to the two world wars— and eventually to the events of the last sixties. These may actually represent the beginning of a "revolution" in consciousness which may come to full maturity at the time of the next opposition between the two planets. Around 2048, Pluto will be in early Pisces and Uranus in early Virgo. Two years later Uranus will have returned to its zodiacal position at Virgo 17°-18°, the degrees that saw the Uranus-Pluto conjunction of 1965-66.

During Teddy Roosevelt's inauguration, Uranus was crossing the Ascendant of the U.S. birth chart; and in 1976 the Presidential elections (just after the Bicentennial celebration) will take place with Neptune crossing that Ascendant. Pluto will reach the same point as the twenty-first century opens. At that time seven planets will be gathered in the zodiacal sign Taurus, repeating a similar congregation also of seven planets in that sign which occurred in 1881 and 1882. However, in May 2000 the three planets Uranus, Neptune, and Pluto will not be in the Taurus area, as Uranus and Neptune will square the planetary stellium from Aquarius. They may be challenging (after a period of chaos and scarcity) a new preoccupation with the acquisition of material resources. The years surrounding the Taurus emphasis of 1881 were marked by an intense effort to colonize Africa in a search for raw materials and new markets.

The Uranus-Neptune Cycle

This cycle lasts about 172 years. We are now in the last phase of the one which began on March 22, 1821 with a conjunction at Capricorn 2°59'; and which will end in 1993, with conjunctions at the 19th and 20th degrees of the same sign. This emphasis on Capricorn, Saturn's essential domain, should be significant as it presumably will not be repeated for many centuries. The year 1821 saw the death of Napoleon I in his St. Helena exile and monarchic reaction dominant in Europe, but not for long. The long opposition between Uranus and Neptune began in 1905 after Uranus entered Capricorn, thus reenergizing the place of the 1821 conjunction. The Russo-Japanese War had started leading to Russia's defeat and aborted revolution. The opposition was in force until Uranus left Capricorn early in 1912. During these seven years pressures were building which led to the Balkan War, Turkey's collapse, and eventually, in 1914, to the murder of the Austrian Archduke at Sarajevo, and World War I.

The "waxing" square of Uranus and Neptune began to operate just after Lincoln's assassination, when Uranus entered Cancer. This was the Reconstruction period, which marked a basic alteration of the character of our nation—an alteration which led to the economic imperialism which began to be displayed as Uranus opposed Neptune under Theodore Roosevelt. The "waning" square between the two planets began around 1950 when Uranus entered Cancer; it became exact in 1953 as Saturn joined Neptune in Libra and lasted until 1957. The Korean War began in 1950; hydrogen bombs were released; Stalin died; Eisenhower was President and Dulles his right hand. The Israel-Egypt War and the crushing of the Hungarian revolt occurred in 1956—and the McCarthy era lasted until 1954.

During the 1965-66 period Neptune was in harmonious sextile to the above-mentioned Uranus-Pluto conjunction; this beneficent influence can be related to the youth movement and the LSD-oriented idealism of the first hippie groups in San Francisco. With all its faults and confusion, that movement may still herald what should be developing sometime next century. On the other hand, the semisquare of Uranus and Neptune coincided with the Watergate affair and the renewed Arab-Israel conflict. Nixon was elected when Uranus at Libra 20° was 44 degrees behind Neptune at Sagittarius 4°—a tense semisquare aspect.

An important fact to consider, if one tries to assess and understand the entire Uranus-Neptune-Pluto process at the present time, is the manner in which each one of these three planets stirs certain important points in a particular chart—for instance, the Mid-Heaven of the U.S. chart at the 3rd degree of Libra. Neptune passed and repassed over that degree during World War II as the atom bomb project was unfolding its world-transforming potentiality. Uranus repeated the transit when Nixon was elected in 1968; and Pluto did the same during the fateful 1972 campaign. As already mentioned, the Ascendant of the U.S. chart will experience the threefold wave of transformative energy in the same order: Neptune crossing the 14th degree of Sagittarius in 1976, Uranus in 1984, Pluto in 2000 or 2001. First comes the Neptunian *dissolution* of obsolete socioeconomic and psychological-personal structures, and the *devaluation* of no longer adequate or relevant ideals; then a Uranian challenge to face reality in a new way follows—a challenge which often takes at first the form of a temporary exaggeration of old desires, fears, and values so that they may be shown pitilessly for what they are. Finally Pluto takes away the glamour surrounding the old images, and exposes the futility and ugliness of what one had so long believed valuable or holy. Seen in this light the coming of Neptune to the Ascendant of the U.S. chart at the time of the national Bicentennial takes on a deeper and somewhat ominous—even if in the end exalting—meaning.[4]

If one wishes to understand as clearly as possible the manner in which the three-pronged process of transformation operates (or rather *should* operate) in a particular birth chart and in a whole life, he should study the positions of Uranus, Neptune, and Pluto in zodiacal signs and Houses, and the aspects they make between

[4] As I am writing this, I notice that a few hours ago there has been a lunar eclipse squared by Jupiter, with the Sun very close to Neptune in Sagittarius (November 29, 1974).

themselves and in relation to Saturn, Jupiter, and the smaller planets. One can also obtain added information by considering the so-called "Arabian" Parts. These are produced by the inter-action of the trans-Saturnian planets as they move along their orbital paths, and by referring these interactions to the four Angles of the birth chart—especially to the Ascendant, but also in the case of public figures, to the Mid-Heaven.

This technique of analysis is rather fascinating; but it should be handled with great care and not given undue importance, as it often refers only to psychological subtleties; yet at times it is most revealing. This is not the place to discuss the matter at great length, and the reader is referred to my book *The Lunation Cycle* for a study of the Parts most often used by astrologers. These Parts are generated by the combined motions of the Moon and the Sun—particularly the Part of Fortune—but any two planets moving at different speed, and therefore whose combined move-ments can be analyzed in terms of their "cycle of relationship," produce Parts when their constantly changing zodiacal positions are referred to the natal horizon and meridian.

If one takes the cycle of relationship produced by the Moon and the Sun, the Moon is the faster-moving celestial body. By adding the longitude of the Moon to that of the Ascendant, and subtracting from the sum the longitude of the Sun, one obtains the longitude of the Part of Fortune. At the conjunction of the Moon and the Sun this Part is quite obviously found conjunct the Ascendant; at Full Moon (opposition aspect) the Part is at the Descendant of the chart. If one considers the birth chart as an unchanging frame of reference, during a complete "lunation cycle" lasting thirty days, the Part of Fortune will move counterclockwise through the first, second, third, etc. Houses and return to the Ascendant at the next New Moon.

However, instead of adding the longitude of the faster body (the Moon) to the Ascendant and subtracting from the sum the longitude of the slower body (the Sun), one can reverse the pro-cedure. What has been called the Part of Spirit (a rather inadequate and confusing term) is produced by adding the Ascendant's and the Sun's longitudes, and subtracting from the sum that of the Moon. This Part is also conjunct the Ascendant at New Moon, and the Descendant at Full Moon, but it moves clockwise passing successively through the twelfth, eleventh, tenth, etc. Houses. Its motion is therefore "retrograde." The Part of Fortune is "direct"; the Part of Spirit, "converse."

One can use exactly the same procedure with Uranus and Neptune, relating the cyclic motion of these two complementary planets to the Ascendant and the Mid-Heaven of a birth chart— the other Angles being less important. What these Parts will reveal in a general way is how the process of transformation operates, or should best operate, in human beings born at any particular phase of the cycle of Uranus-Neptune relationship. Persons born just after 1821 had the Part close to their Ascendant— if one studies this Part referred to that Angle. People born from 1903 to 1912 had these Parts in their sixth or seventh Houses because Uranus and Neptune were coming to or past their opposition. Any particular generation can thus be characterized according to this technique. In the generation born *before* the Uranus-Neptune opposition, and therefore having the direct Part in their sixth House, the tendency to *exteriorize* the transformative process through sixth House activities (work, service, health matters, retraining, etc.) should have been in evidence. In the people born *after* the opposition this same tendency should have been focused in the field of close relationship: partnership, social association, class, and color problems, etc. (the seventh House).

Yet while the *direct* Part "exteriorizes" the combined effect of Uranus and Neptune, the *retrograde* Part "interiorizes" this effect. What this means in most cases is that the position of the direct Part in a natal House points to the type of experience through which the process of transformation is most likely to, and should most effectively, operate. In the U.S. chart—which refers to our entire nation as a "collective person"—this Part is in the eighth House (Leo 29°34')—the House of business (as business is the fruition of human association and contracts) and also that of sharing in depth collective experiences (thus rituals, baseball games, the rituals of business, group-feelings). In 1776 this Part was close to the great star Regulus, which is associated with political power and in general with the keynote of the Piscean Age. Now that Regulus (by precessional motion) is at Leo 29°27′ it has come even closer to an exact conjunction.

On the other hand, the *retrograde* Uranus-Neptune Part usually points to the direction in which one longs for being, and one can best become, identified *in consciousness* (i.e., internally) with a larger whole and involved in it—for better or for worse. In the U.S. chart this Part at Pisces 26°46′ falls in the third House—a House dealing with the environment and all manners of communication processes, which in turn involve skill and cunning or cleverness in building and making use of such processes. In the chart of ex-President Nixon, born in 1913 after the opposition of Uranus to Neptune, his direct Uranus-Neptune Part is in the House of partnership and conflict-solving (the lawyer's skill); while his retrograde Uranus-Neptune Part fell in the House of work, service, health, and personal crises or retraining. In my own birth chart the direct Part, at Taurus 20° is in exact opposition to my real natal Uranus, thus stressing a Uranian character and destiny, further emphasized by the fact that my natal horizon is nearly identical with Uranus' nodal axis (heliocentric nodes). The converse Part, at Cancer 7°, falls in the seventh House, thus giving a transformative importance to new ideals of interpersonal relationship.

In some cases at least, the Sabian Symbols of the zodiacal degrees on which these Parts occur prove very significant. In my chart, the direct Part's degree is symbolized by *"Wisps of wing-like clouds streaming across the sky*—The awareness of spiritual forces at work ... the blessing of supernatural forces"; and the symbol for the converse Part by *"Two nature spirits dancing under the Moonlight*—The play of invisible forces in all manifestations of life.... Creative imagination."

In Nixon's chart, the symbol for the direct Part (the 23rd degree of Pisces) is:

> "*A materializing medium giving a séance*— The person who believes he or she has a mission or mandate . . . must substantiate his belief. He has to produce results. . . . It always demands to some extent the gift of some power or value which is deeply one's own. . . . The medium's psychic substance provides the materials visible in the phenomena if the latter are genuine. After the séance, the medium is usually exhausted. The performer gives his very life to the performance. . . . The display of psychic power . . . can be interpreted positively or negatively according to the motives that induced the 'medium' to give the séance." (*An Astrological Mandala*, p. 283.)

This might substantiate the belief that one of the aspects of Nixon's destiny, or karma, was to reveal glaringly what could be wrong in the recent trend to exalt and glorify the executive function in our government.

The symbol for Nixon's converse Part (the 7th degree of Pisces in the sixth House) is: "*Illumined by a shaft of light, a large cross lies on rocks surrounded by sea mist.*" This symbol can be given the positive interpretation of "the spiritual blessing which strengthens individuals who, happen what may, stand uncompromisingly for their own truth." But it can also refer to the inner loneliness of a man who carries as a cross an inner ideal he is not able to actualize, just because of inner complexes and a crude will for "self-assertion." (*An Astrological Mandala*, p. 272.) [5]

In other cases the midpoint between Uranus and Neptune can also be of great significance—and also those between Uranus and Pluto, and Neptune and Pluto. The value of midpoints has recently been highly emphasized, but in many instances perhaps too much so. They are said to be "sensitive points" at which the radiations from two planets are interrelated in a focalized man-

---

[5] It should be clear that such symbols can only be used when the moment of the first breath (thus the exact degree of the Ascendant) is known.

ner; and if another planet is found at such points, natally or by transit, a further combination and emphasis is said to occur. As two midpoints (in opposition to each other) can be calculated for each two planets—or even for the Angles—a large number of these points exist. In Nixon's chart the midpoints between Uranus and Neptune are located at the 29th degrees of Aries and Libra; thus, in square to the two planets, because they are in near opposition. They fall in the eighth and second Houses, involving money and business—important matters for a young man with the ineradicable ambition to play a dominant role in the greater whole his nation (and even mankind) represents for him.

If one could find a way of at least symbolically synthesizing the activities of Uranus, Neptune, and Pluto and focalizing the result upon one constantly moving point, he would have a perhaps very valuable clue to the way the whole threefold process of world-transformation is unfolding its potentiality. Several possibilities suggest themselves, but I would not vouch for the validity of any of them. The simplest and most obvious would be to add the longitudes of the three planets and to divide the sum by three. When the three planets are in exact conjunction—granted that this ever happens—the point resulting from this operation (which I shall call the Point of Transformation) would fall on the degree of that triple conjunction. As the planets separate, each moving at its own rhythm, the zodiacal longitude of this Point constantly changes, advancing gradually, but falling back when one of the three planets pass from longitude 360 to longitude 1.

Logically, when planets like Jupiter and Saturn are found conjunct this Point of Transformation, some more or less definite results should be experienced—or at least a clue should be made available as to the meaning of what is happening. The position of this Point in a birth chart is often quite important as an indication of the overall character and effectiveness of the process of transformation in that individual's life. In both cases, the symbol of the degree of the Point of Transformation quite often proves significant. I shall give a few examples.

On the day of the assassination of the Austrian Archduke, June 28, 1914, which precipitated World War I, Pluto was at 0°47′ Cancer, Neptune at 27°07′ Cancer, and Uranus at 10°55′ Aquarius. Adding these three longitudes and dividing the sum by three gives 173° or Virgo 23°—a degree symbolized by *A Lion Tamer*. The symbol seems significant even if what happened was that the lion ate the man supposed to tame it! Particularly interesting is the fact that in the U.S. birth chart Neptune in the ninth House (diplomacy, travel, foreign involvement) is located on that same degree. The Point of Transformation on that day of June was squaring Saturn at Gemini 23½° which is very close to the U.S. Mars degree in the House of War and Alliances (the seventh House).

When the armistice ended the war (November 11, 1918, 5:00 A.M. at Senlis, France), the Point of Transformation had reached the 4th degree of Libra (Symbol: *"Around a campfire a group of young people sit in spiritual communion:* The necessity to unite with kindred spirits as one enters unbeaten paths. . . . The urge to create a new society and respond to new values . . . for the reception of creative inspiration."*) The League of Nations' ideal fits well the Libra position; and quite significantly this Point had passed over the U.S. chart's Mid-Heaven during America's participation in the war, a participation inspired by our President, Woodrow Wilson, in the name of a great ideal of peace and world-unity; alas, only an ideal scorned by the political and economic realities of the day. The President signed the Declaration of War on April 6, 1917 as the Point reached the last degree of Virgo symbolized as follows: *"Totally intent upon completing an immediate task, a man is deaf to any allurement*—Total concentration."

In late October 1929, at the time of the big stock-market crash which ushered in the Depression for our country, the Point of Transformation was at Cancer 4½°, Uranus having recently entered Aries, moving through the fourth House of the U.S. chart. Saturn was about to enter Capricorn, opposing the Point of Transformation and squaring Uranus throughout the winter of 1930. Significantly, Cancer $4\frac{1}{2}°$ is very close to the exact midpoint of the Venus-Jupiter conjunction in the U.S. chart, located in the seventh House. That House deals with all forms of social associations, contracts, and partnerships; and the sign Cancer represents the home and its security. Hundreds of thousands of homes had to be abandoned because of the owners' inability to pay the mortgages. The symbol for the 5th degree of Cancer significantly fits the general situation which caused the Depression: "*At a railroad crossing an automobile is wrecked by a train*—The tragic results which are likely to occur when the individual will pits itself carelessly against the power of the collective will of society . . . karmic readjustment." The Depression was indeed the collective karma of a Western civilization which had apparently learned nothing from the tragedy of the first world war.

When Hitler invaded Poland in September 1939, the Point of Transformation was on the 6th degree of Leo—the sign of dictatorial power—and getting close to the U.S. Moon's North Node. The symbol of that degree pictures a blatantly modern girl challenging a conservative old lady; and World War II with its advanced technology and atom bomb represented indeed the challenge of a future society to the old European system and the neotribalism of the Nazi ideology. Saturn was then entering Taurus and squared the Point of Transformation as Germany invaded France.

Pearl Harbor occurred on December 7, 1941, around 8:00 A.M. as Pluto had reached Leo 5°35′, Neptune Virgo 29°42′ (the longitude of the Point of Transformation when U.S. entered World War I!), and Uranus Taurus 27°38′. The Point of Transformation was then at the 11th degree of Leo in the eighth House of the U.S. chart. Its symbol seems less adequate as it refers to young children's dependence upon a great tradition for their play-activity, but actually the war had already started, and the Pearl Harbor tragedy unified all Americans around their common national source of power—and perhaps war remains the "play" of men who mentally are still children.

An interesting phase of the three-sided Uranus-Neptune-Pluto interrelationship developed during most of the second world war, because Uranus and Neptune formed a constantly shifting trine aspect, with Pluto moving near their midpoint in the early degree of Leo. This configuration began in the spring of 1940 when Hitler invaded France and nearly defeated England, as Neptune late in Virgo was moving back and forth over the place it occupied in July 4, 1776, in the ninth House (foreign affairs) of the U.S. birth chart. Uranus was then passing through the third decanate (20 to 30 degrees) of Taurus. On the day of the Pearl Harbor attack, Uranus and Neptune were still respectively in Virgo and Taurus. A year later, when the first controlled atomic reaction occurred in Chicago under the physicist Fermi's direction, Neptune had moved to Libra 2° and Uranus to Gemini 2°; thus forming an exact trine, while Pluto at Leo was near their midpoint and in broad sextile to both. As a result, the Point of Transformation was at Leo 4° nearly conjunct Pluto.

One might infer from this eminently harmonious configuration linking the three trans-Saturnian planets, that they cooperated closely in the process of transformation, however drastic its results were at the human level. The energy or influence generated by their "perfect chord" could be said to have been released symmetrically through the zodiacal region opposite the Point of Transformation, thus around Aquarius 4°. The interesting fact was that President Franklin D. Roosevelt had his natal Venus at Aquarius 6° and his Sun at Aquarius 11°08′. He had Pluto at Taurus 27°22′ (which Uranus was transiting as he strove to prepare a rather reluctant America for what he realized was an impending war) and Uranus and his Ascendant at about Virgo 18° (a degree transited by Neptune during 1937-38 when Hitler was moving forward in Austria). He was thus, astrologically speaking, the "man of the hour." The same Uranus-Neptune-Pluto configuration was still effective when the United Nations organization came to be an official reality after Russia's ratification. At the time (October 24, 1945) the Moon was conjunct Uranus, and Venus on the same degree as Neptune. Jupiter was just ahead in

Libra and about to transit the U.S. natal Saturn. The point opposite Pluto 'was F. D. Roosevelt's Sun—a "coincidence" indeed!

When President Nixon was elected in November 1968, Uranus was crossing the U.S. Mid-Heaven, and the Point of Transformation was located at Libra 18°. It had been passing over the U.S. Saturn in the tenth House (the Executive) during the Presidential campaign! The symbol for the 18th degree of Libra is rather startling, in view of what ocurred after Watergate: *"Two men placed under arrest."* This shows the result of a "breakdown in the relationship between the individual and society" and "the fact that *two* men are pictured under arrest suggests a polarization and a purpose transcending a merely personal fit of recklessness"— and Nixon was elected for two terms! The keyword for the degree is given as "facing the consequences." (Cf. *An Astrological Mandala,* pp. 183 and 184.)

If we look at Nixon's birth chart we find that the Point of Transformation is located at Virgo 19°, in his first House and some 6 degrees from his Ascendant on the 14th degree. The symbol for Virgo 19° is befitting: *"A swimming race:* The stimulation that comes from a group effort toward a spiritual goal . . . the personal ego-centered ambitions to succeed and to be 'first' is indeed a sign of expectable spiritual failure."

The Point of Transformation at the time of President Ford's inauguration was located at the 4th degree of Scorpio symbolized by *"A youth carrying a lighted candle in a devotional ritual:* The educative power of ceremonies which impress the great images of a culture upon its gathered participants." Perhaps also a befitting symbol for our new President upon whose shoulders a responsibility was placed which he was barely prepared to assume.

Whatever the validity of such a technique may prove to be when adequately tested, it shows at least the possibility of synthesizing in one point the threefold operation of the process of transformation and of evoking its focused significance at specific times and in the chart of an individual person who is particularly affected by the process. Astrology is a field rich in possibilities for inventing myriad techniques to deal with the immense complexity of human situations and needs. Each astrologer—like each psychologist—naturally gravitates toward the kind of procedures which are in tune with his basic temperament. The character of the types of psychology developed by Freud, Adler, Jung, and Assagioli, is clearly shown in the birth chart of each of these men. A man's creations are projections of what he archetypally is. Truth is susceptible of infinite variations, for it has to meet the particular needs of all particular phases of mankind's long evolution, of all particular persons, and all particular situations. Spirit is universal in its transcendent essence, but it reaches a focal manifestation only in particular situations. The divine is immanent in the personal. It operates in whatever is able to transform the person on his or her way toward an open-ended and ever more inclusive consciousness of the scope, power, and meaning of existence.

PART THREE

·7·

A Transphysical Approach to the Galaxy

In order to understand the full implications of what is here called a galactic approach to astrology—and by extension to psychology and the many forms of social organization—we have to return to the concept of a dialectic sequence of three great evolutionary periods in the development of consciousness: the *archaic*, the *classical*, and the *holarchic* periods. We are witnessing today mankind's slow and hesitant passage from the classical to the holarchic stage of consciousness; and it is as disturbing a process as that which transformed the archaic and early tribal type of awareness and approach to Nature into an individualistic and rationalistic consciousness, centered around the feeling-experience of being "I." This transformation is far from being universally achieved, especially in its positive aspect, and it has produced a peculiar and inherently tragic cleavage between what is regarded as a higher and lower development of the potential of consciousness innate in every human being. The ideas expressed in this book and in several of my previous works open up the possibility of healing such a cleavage without implying the necessity of returning to the archaic attitude of man toward life and the instinctual bio-psychic energies operating at the level of the biosphere.

In his archaic state of consciousness—whatever may be the physical and social facts of existence related to it—primitive man is enfolded by what, at a later period, will be called "Nature." He exists within the biospheric womb of the Earth-mother, moved by her life-rhythms to which his inner psychic being is just as closely attuned as his physical body. Man is able to survive because of a remarkable capacity for adaptation due to such physical factors as special hands, an erect spine, and a particularly sensitive nervous system. He also has even at that early stage, a mind capable of relating experienced facts, or generalizing from those facts, and, by means of symbolic gestures and sounds, of communicating his experiences to other human beings. He is endowed—perhaps uniquely—with the ability to interpret what he perceives in terms of some frame of reference from which he derives a sense of order.

Any concept of order arises either out of the interpretation of a deep and lasting feeling of order in the sequence of experienced events, or as a psychically necessary compensation for what at first seems to be unrelated, disordered, and unexplainable sequences of events. As primitive man was faced with what appeared to him as two basic realms of events—events which took place on an Earth of which he could only experience small and seemingly flat areas, and events of a totally different character which occurred on the dome of the sky—he came to the inevitable conclusion that in actual fact there were two worlds: the obscure and damp realm of jungles, forests, or swamps filled with unpredictable dangers, and the realm of the sky in which points and discs of light moved regularly and predictably on the mysterious background of the empty darkness of celestial space.

Considering what we know of the conditions prevailing on the Earth's surface, when mankind developed at a more-than-animal level of consciousness some millions of years ago, it is evident that man's first and most basic feeling-experience was one of almost complete subservience to the Earth-mother and to her energies in which he bodily shared. He felt the impact and inner compulsion of these life energies directly and forcefully, and he was swayed by their dark power. Yet whether it was when the deep fogs surrounding the flat Earth lifted, or when groups of men began to live in the open spaces of semidesertic regions through which great rivers—the Nile, the Euphrates, the Ganges, the Yellow River of China—flowed, a moment came when the contemplation of the clear sky and the study of celestial motions assumed a basic importance, particularly in terms of agriculture and cattle raising. This sky had two aspects: a day aspect and a night aspect. The Sun totally dominated the former, while the latter revealed the movements of the Moon and the stars. Some of these stars became known as "planets" (meaning, wanderers) because of their erratic movements; others were eventually called "fixed," not because they did not move nightly and seasonally, but because they kept fixed distances between them.

Because the Sun appeared to be the source of heat and of light, capable of raising crops from the soil in the annual miracle of the rebirth of vegetation, this Sun became the central figure in the world of the sky. At the same time, the human male was taking an increasingly dominant role in tribal life, not only because of his muscular strength, but because of his ability to discover new ways of living, new processes in agriculture and in warfare. Such achievements very likely caused some especially gifted men to feel superior and different. This superiority and difference was at first interpreted as due to their being in "special" communication either with the life energies of the Earth-mother, or with celestial gods—or (in some societies) as being direct descendants of gods having long ago incarnated as men.

Eventually, when the Sun was worshipped as ruler of the sky and "Father" of celestial gods who had become related to the path upon which he journeyed each year through the sky, the zodiac, the concept of a "solar hero," developed. The solar hero was a man who had become like the Sun in his life and his deeds. As the Sun was the center of all the activities belonging to the conscious aspect of life—the day period—so the man who in his

community was radiant and creative like a Sun could feel himself, and was venerated by others, as the center of the day activities
of his social world. He occupied a unique role; he was the "one
and only" Sun—at least while he lived. He assumed the role of
Father to the tribe which he may have saved from disaster. From
patriarchal ruler of a small tribe, he eventually became a godlike
king around whom a complex society and its culture revolved.
Eventually, the privileges once reserved for the solar hero or king
were assumed to be the birthrights of every man. "Every man a
king" was the political motto of a famous American demagogue.
Tribal man had become transformed into an individual person,
theoretically responsible, self-motivated, and centered in consciousness around an "inner Ruler."

What is implied in this process of individualization is the spread
of the concept of *centrality*. This concept has been given many
forms, religious, psychological, social. In the Orient, it became
symbolized and pictured in the mandala. But the mandala as a
symbol of human integration can be traced to the idea of the
universal king, the *Chakravartin,* the ideal monarch before whom
all lesser kings have to bow, and for whom mankind was a vast
mandala of which he was the all-conquering, all-integrating and
perfectly just, center.[1] It is on this concept that the Classical approach to existence and to the universe is based; and this approach
found its expression in the heliocentric system—one radiant central Sun around which a group of dark planets revolve, reflecting
as best they can its multifarious power.

The development of a heliocentric system and the growth of
individualism in the Western world were synchronous processes.
They were made possible by a special kind of development of the
mind. Intellectual faculties of observation and analysis, plus a
degree of inventiveness and skill, were required to make a clear
and convincing heliocentric picture of the universe. Likewise, an
active mind and the particular type of language it had built were

[1] Cf. Heinrich Zimmer, *Philosophies of India* (New York: Meridian Books),
pp. 127–139.

needed in order to formulate, justify, and generalize the first intuitions (or feeling-experiences) of the existence in us of a centralizing and sustaining self to which every sensation, feeling, and thought-process could be referred.

The moment one speaks of "center" one is faced with new problems: What is the nature of the contents of the circle implied in the idea of center? What kind of center is it? The hub of a wheel is also a center, but, in a sense, it refers to empty space. On the other hand, according to the heliocentric theory, the center of the solar system is an enormous mass of energy-matter, dwarfing the size of the other components of the system. Unlike the central solar masses, these components are dark material globes. Thus such a picture of the solar system can be used symbolically to characterize and unconsciously to justify groups of entities in which the central one possesses most of the power of the group and radiates it upon the others who are deprived of power and totally subjected to the attraction of the massive and glowing center. Translated to the language of social organization, the heliocentric system justifies any totalitarian grouping, even though it implies that the central individual should be a beneficent paternalistic autocrat!

The reader might protest that the solar system is actually what the modern astronomer has pictured, after an enormous amount of careful measurements. However this is not a valid objection, because this astronomical picture owes its existence to the astronomer, who is a human being endowed with senses of a particular type, with a mind able to invent a particular kind of material instrument providing a certain type of data which he systematizes according to a certain basic assumption or postulate. Any living being is faced with a universe that answers to his need as an evolving organized system of consciousness and material energy. The Copernican Revolution came at the exact time when Renaissance man was developing a new type of individualistic self-assertion, and large human collectivities were being ruthlessly organized into national states dominated by powerful kings who "by divine right" possessed the entire country upon which they autocratically ruled.

This is why I called that stage in the evolution of human consciousness the classical period. It was dominated by twin concepts: *centrality* and *rationality*. These concepts were presumably developed during the classical period of Greek culture some twenty-five centuries ago, with probable antecedents in the short-lived reform of the Egyptian pharaoh, Akhnaton, and in the also actually short-lived experience of Moses, whose initial vision of God as the "I am that I am" was apparently at once deviated so as to adjust to tribal conditions which the vision could not supplant (no more than Woodrow Wilson's dream of world peace through international union could supplant the old patterns of national sovereignty and cultural pride).

With very few exceptions, centrality still means for human minds a concentration of power at the center; and such a concentration of power at the social-political level (or at the psychological level of will) in most cases produces drastic and often tragic results. As to the concept of "rationality," it is usually identified with an Aristotelian type of logic based on the principle of exclusion (no two objects can occupy the same place at the same time) and on the premise that the laws of our material universe apply everywhere at all times independently of who the observer is. Some aspects of these two principles have been developed much further by European thinkers from the fifteenth to the twentieth centuries; but recently new concepts have begun to undermine some of the old premises or paradigms. Still, the intellectual framework which these produced remains standing with an official stamp of authority, for the simple reason that it is still needed by human beings, having pushed to an extreme along materialistic lines the concept of individualism and individual rights.

What I am attempting to do here is to transform the concept of centrality by introducing a new one, that of *galacticity*. Properly defined in terms of a true fourth dimension whose keynote (as already stated) is *interpenetration,* this new concept would also transform the special kind of rationalism which our Western civilization has produced. Why the term "galacticity"? Because the emerging picture of our Galaxy, if interpreted in a new way, could provide us with a symbolic celestial representation of a type of human organization which is also beginning to emerge in the consciousness of a few future-oriented and truly creative thinkers—just as the picture of the heliocentric system provided classical cultures with an appropriate symbol of *the higher possibilities* of a paternalistic totalitarian type of religious and socio-political-cultural organization.

As already indicated, the transition from centrality to galacticity can be made by realizing that our Sun is also one of billions of stars within the Galaxy. This is the key realization. When man's proud and possessive feeling of "being I"—a feeling which seeks to perpetuate and reproduce itself by any available means—gives way to the realization that this "I" is but one of a multitude of component parts within the "greater whole" of humanity; when, moreover, man's consciousness begins to operate in terms of concepts related to "light," rather than of the material values associated with existence on dark planets—then, the transition can be successfully made. It will lead man's consciousness from the third-dimensional realm of planetary materiality to a fourth-dimensional space in which all light-centers interpenetrate. It will lead to the truly holistic and hierarchic (thus "holarchic") stage of human evolution.

Modern astronomy as yet knows very little about the constitution of the Galaxy as a whole. The larger stars we see with the naked eye are relatively close to our solar system in terms of astronomical distances. Clouds of dark matter apparently hide from our sight the core of the Galaxy which is located in the direction of the constellation Sagittarius. Interpreted in terms of geocentric longitude, the galactic center at present is located at Sagittarius 26°30′. Astronomers nevertheless have deduced from long and

careful observations that the Galaxy is a spiral system of stars
and star-groups. It also contains vast "clouds" of hydrogen and
many other substances scattered through the immense field of
activity it covers. This galactic spiral seems to have five arms (a
significant number in view of the archetypal meaning of No. 5
which refers to mental-spiritual processes) and the solar system
is at the inner edge of the Orion arm, the third one from the
core of the Galaxy. The Sun is about 27,000 or more *light-years*
from that galactic core (a light-year corresponds, in terms of distance, to about 5.8 trillion miles). The diameter of the whole
Galaxy is now estimated to be more than 100,000 light-years; and
the Sun appears to revolve around the galactic "center"—whatever it be—in 200 millions of our earthly years, though the exact
path it is following is as yet not determined. It is moving in the
direction of the constellation Hercules; and its motion at present
points to what, in geocentric celestial longitude, is a point at
2°06′ of Capricorn.[2]

From his particular position inside of the Galaxy and far away
from its center, it is extremely difficult for man to make a clear
picture of this vast cosmic whole of which our solar system is
a very small part. We can only perceive with any degree of clarity
whatever is contained within a relatively very small section of
the whole in which, *in actual and concrete fact,* we "live, move
and have our being." The following sketch will give a general
idea of the structure of the Galaxy as we are able to imagine it
at present. What we know of the Galaxy constitutes only a very
small area around the Sun. The star closest to our solar system,
Alpha Centaurus, is 4 light-years (over 25 trillions of miles) distant from us.

The general spiralic form of our Galaxy is not a unique occurrence in the cosmos. There may be in our universe billions
of star-systems, also confusingly named galaxies, though the word
"Galaxy" (literally meaning "Milky Way") should be reserved

2 Cf. Dr. Theodor Landscheidt, *Cosmic Cybernetics* (Aalen, Germany:
1973).

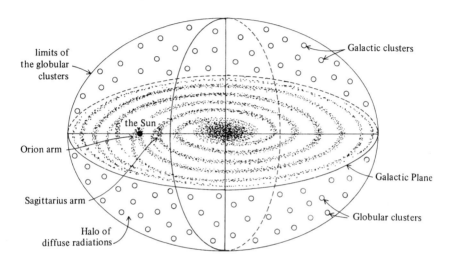

Perspective View of the Galaxy

The "Auric Egg" of the Galaxy

Our Sun is in the third arm at about 30,000 light-years from the center. (Orion Arm)

Astronomy by Donald H. Menzel [New York: Random House, p. 255.]

to the "island universe" of which our solar system is a part. One of them, the Andromeda galaxy, is larger than ours, and is turned toward us in such a way that we can get a most beautiful picture of its overall structure, which presumably resembles ours. It is assumed that its distance from us is from 1,600,000 to 2,500,000 light-years; but we are now able to detect the presence of star-systems at least two-hundred times further away.

Star-systems occur in what astronomers call "clusters." Our Galaxy is part of a small cluster of seventeen such star systems— the Galaxy and the Andromeda system being diametrically opposed within an elliptical space whose longest apsis must have a length corresponding to 2 million or more light-years. Much more "populated" clusters of perhaps one thousand members have been discovered within many sections of the sky but incredibly farther away than the stars ordinarily associated with the traditional constellations. A cluster in the constellation Ursus Major is 700 million light-years away from us, and more distant ones are being discovered.

Such distances hardly make any sense; they can be conceived only as numerical abstractions. It is true that they can be reduced to a more understandable size, and all books attempting to popularize the recent discoveries of astronomers have done so, but this procedure does not solve the real problem which is: What do we mean by distance? Put differently, the question becomes even more significant: What do we mean by space?

In my book *The Planetarization of Consciousness* [3] I stated that we can only truly understand space in terms of relationship. The concept of space is abstracted from the actual experience of relationship. Two objects that are related appear to be in space, in the sense that they are at some distance from each other. This is why the principle of exclusion in classical logic states that two objects cannot occupy the same space at the same time. If there are two coexisting physical objects there must be space between

[3] Published in 1971, and now in a paperback edition (Harper and Row, N.Y.).

them, however infinitesimally small the distance between them may be. An infinitely *extensive* space is required to account for an infinite number of relationships. Conversely, if there are no relationships—that is, if the universe is in a state of absolute unity ("one without a second" as the Hindu Vedanta describes Brahman)—space is reduced to the mathematical point, a point without dimension.

Space therefore should be thought of as oscillating between a limited state of infinite extension and one of no-dimensionality, the mathematical point. In theory, neither state can ever be reached; just as in Chinese philosophy, Yang never completely overpowers Yin; or Yin, Yang. To say this, however, does not imply that space is the expression of one and only one kind of relationship. This is where the concept of multidimensionality comes in. One-dimensional space refers to a particular type of relatedness—that is, to linear relationships. Two-dimensional space refers to relationships having length and width; three-dimensional space, to the kind of relationships which we interpret as occurring among objects, persons, and other *physically material* entities. A true four-dimensional space would refer to relationships associating entities that exist in a *transphysical* state of materiality. In this state, all entities essentially "interpenetrate."

The concept of interpenetration can be illustrated in several ways. Think of the experience of hearing music performed by a symphony orchestra whose players are hidden from sight. If, as trained musicians, we know that the orchestral sounds come from various instruments constituting physically separate sources— thus existing in physical space—we can identify the tones of trumpets, violins, flutes, or timpani. Yet what our ears actually and directly perceive is a series of complex sounds. At any moment of the performance only one sound reaches our auditory center, complex as that sound may be. It is a compound tone in which a number of sound waves—of fundamentals, overtones, and beat-tones—blend in a unified sensation. In other words, the tones produced by the many instruments of the orchestra interpenetrate. They are related in a four-dimensional state in which, to the ear that perceives them, there is no distance in terms of *physical extension.* If a sensation of distance is produced in the consciousness of the hearer, it is because of the stereo effect produced by the fact that he has two ears, or because he has learned intellectually to separate the different qualities of the components of the compound tone he hears.

A scientist-philosopher, Donald Hatch Andrews, a few years ago wrote a book entitled *The Symphony of Life* (Lee Summit, Mo.: Unity Books, 1966) in which he stated that "the universe is composed not of matter, but of music"; and the great physicist, Erwin Schrödinger, ended his oft-quoted small volume, *What Is Life?* by the challenging statement that what we know of the universe gives it the character of mind rather than that of what we traditionally understand as matter. Schrödinger also stresses the fact that what we actually observe is "form" (gestalt) and that "the habit of everyday language deceives us when it makes us believe that form must be the shape or form of *something*" and "that a material substratum is required to take on a shape" (*Science and Humanism* [Cambridge, England: Cambridge University Press, 1952], p. 21).

Following such a trend of thought, could we not say that space is relationship, or more precisely, the state of relatedness; and that we need not think of "entities" being related "in" space? Rather it is *space that, by vibrating, produces what appear to our consciousness as entities.* These entities—including human beings, with their feeling of centrality and individuality—are the results of interferences produced by the interplay of "space-vibrations." Thus, one may consider material entities not as "things" that vibrate "in" space, but as the products of the immensely complex vibratory state of space itself. Because the interplay of these space-vibrations occurs at various vibratory levels—each level referring to a characteristic mode of relatedness—we generally speak of three fundamental levels or modes of relatedness, which we call matter, mind, and spirit. Matter, mind, and spirit are the three most characteristic modes of existence traditionally conceived by our human consciousness. It may be that man can only imagine these three essential modes, immensely varied though their manifestations actually are.

It has been said that architecture is frozen music. In a similar sense, one could state that matter is "frozen" mind. In one of its main aspects, mind is matter-oriented; it is close to its freezing point. In another aspect, it is spirit-oriented and reaching to a state of incandescence or, as is traditionally said, "illumined." To man's consciousness spirit manifests as light. Light is a mode of vibration of space, and for man's consciousness it represents or symbolizes *the state of relatedness which we call spirit.*

Spirit is the state of "perfect relatedness." [4] The consciousness illumined by spirit "sees" the entire universe as all-encompassing Harmony—as a perfect Chord in which all vibrations blend. In this Chord space is "fulfilled" as a *pleroma* of vibrations. It is also a plenitude of consciousness, for consciousness is another term for relatedness. Where there is relationship, there also is consciousness; and as there are levels of relationship, there are also levels of consciousness—material, mental, and spiritual.

In the same sense, we should think of "form" at three basic levels of existence or perception: in terms of *matter* (material bodies); of *mind* ("concepts" which are abstractions of data of experience in the world of matter, and "ideas" which reflect conditions existing at the level of spirit-relatedness); and of *spirit*— the principle of form at the level of spirit operating in terms of what human consciousness calls Archetypes, Numbers, Platonic Ideas, etc.

The reader may regard the foregoing as purely metaphysical speculation. But any culture is based upon such metaphysical ideas. There can be no radical transformation of long taken-for-

---

[4] Tantric Hindu philosophy refers to the ultimate human achievement as the "Perfect Experience"—in Sanskrit, *Purna* (cf. the well-known books of Sri Woodruff on the tantra).

granted ideas and mental pictures or basic feelings—like the feeling of being an isolated, self-sufficient, and irreducible "I"—unless new metaphysical concepts are born within a spiritually illumined consciousness. They arise as deep intuitive realizations of the imperative *need* to transcend the institutionalized pattern of the collective mentality characteristic of a society that has reached its autumnal phase of disintegration. These intuitions, or seed ideas, must be given a consistent, and—at least for minds that are open and eager for new light—convincing, mental formulation. All the new cosmological theories of modern astrophysics are essentially metaphysical formulations, even though they are anchored, often precariously and always uncertainly, upon the "facts" revealed by our even more complex and far-seeing instruments. What is needed today in our scientific age is a transphysical rather than a strictly metaphysical formulation.

Astrology itself has no basically valid meaning except as the practical application of an implied metaphysics. Unfortunately the ordinary astrologer is as unaware of, or uninterested in such a metaphysical foundation as the ordinary college-graduated technician is aware of, and interested in the metaphysical concepts of scientifically oriented philosophers and of the new group of "philosophers of science." Even those serious astrologers who are most eager to be of help to their clients, are often not deeply concerned with the questions of *what* astrology really implies, *why* it works, and *how* its use might psychologically affect the users. Again, they do not differ in this from technologists intent on making their inventions ever more effective, with no great concern as to what use their society will make of them—even, in fact, when it is quite evident that, in this present state of society, the invention will be used for destructive purposes.

As traditional astrology in most instances deals with events referring to the relationship between human beings acting on a material environment, it operates at the level where planets move as dark and solid masses of matter within what we picture as the heliocentric system. Even the central Sun at that level is seen as a mass of matter in a state of extreme heat which makes it a source of intense radiations. These radiations are interpreted as "particles" (photons), though they also ambiguously appear to behave as "waves." This ambivalence can be related to the double character of "Sun" and "star."

This dualism provides us with a symbolic key to a clear understanding of the possibility of raising our consciousness of what constitutes reality from the level of *centralized materiality* to that of *galacticity*. It tells us symbolically what is the next step in this process of transcendence (I do not use the term *transcendence* in an absolute sense—as when the Christian philosopher speaks of God as "the absolute Other" and establishes an absolute separation between God the Creator and man the creature—but only as meaning a "stepping through" the long-accepted but no longer exclusively acceptable limitations of the state of *physicality*).

It seems logical and indeed inevitable symbolically to associate the transphysical level of consciousness with the concept of galacticity, because the Galaxy now presents to man's mind the new challenge to its capacity for cosmic imagining. But this challenge is not met when we consider galactic stars in the same (at least relatively) materialistic way in which astronomy pictures our Sun. The two conditions of "Sun" and "star" should not be approached by our minds as if they existed at the same level. When man's mind is hypnotized by the physicality of his dark, unradiating planetary environment, he can only picture the Sun as a physical mass of extremely hot matter, and its power as resulting from nuclear reactions which we seem able to duplicate.

If we insist on remaining at the level of dark planets in need of a centralizing source of cosmic energy we may assume that this astrophysical picture is "true"—or, we should better say, adequate or valid. Still we should accept at least the possibility that the Sun, as a star participating in the vast wholeness of the Galaxy, operates at another level of existence where physical matter becomes *transsubstantiated* into music and mind. The rationale for such a transsubstantiation is to be found in the concept of space which has been outlined in the simplest terms in the preceding pages.

The Galaxy, according to this transphysical picture, is conceived as a pleroma of light-forms produced by the interplay of space-vibrations. The stars are the "children" of space itself, when space is set in whirling motion. They are condensations of light-space—or spirit—in *formal relationship* to each other. It is a formal relationship which, as I see it, does not obey the principles of centrality and rationality or exclusion. By this I mean that the galactic center is not occupied by an enormous mass of matter like a super-Sun, but could be better compared to the hub of a wheel. At the galactic core the cosmic force which in our physical world of dark planets we call gravitation—or its galactic analogue—must be condensed or concentrated. At this core, which may be what recently astronomers have thought of as a "white hole," spirit may surge outward from a higher dimension or possibly another universe.

This does not mean that the astronomers' tentative picture of the Galaxy and of clusters of various types of galactic star-systems is not valid. Theirs is an interpretation of what they perceive, when they carefully analyze the different testimonies of their instruments. But we can also interpret the facts as referring to the *materialized reflection* of "forms of vibratory relationship," forms that at the galactic level have a character transcending the nature of the relationships between each of the physical entities we observe at our planetary Earth-level of existence.

It will probably be said that if our consciousness is not able to operate at the level of "galacticity," it is useless for us to think in terms basically foreign to our awareness of "materiality"; but if this were a valid objection, then there would be no sense for men ever to proclaim *ideals* which we expect to act as determinants in our individual or collective living. There would then be no sense in any religious beliefs.

Archaic man interpreted the stars as the radiant bodies of gods. Modern scientists think of them as enormous masses of matter in the plasma state, within which unimaginably powerful chemicoatomic reactions take place. Each picture fits the particular level of the collective consciousness of the men who believe it to be "true." Each picture is adequate in terms of the collective human *need* which it is meant to answer. In a classical culture (especially in our classical European culture) men who, for a long time, had their collective mentality utterly conditioned by religious dogmas based on some assumed divine revelation, reacted to such a conditioning by developing a more analytical, objective, or empirical kind of mind. The nature of that mind made it especially apt at dealing with the world in terms of "materiality." It also produced, or was associated in man with a deeply stirring feeling of "centrality." As a result man increasingly operated in terms of egocentric impulses which he socially idealized as inborn rights, and justified as evidence of an immanent "divine" center, theoretically able to rule over the disparate elements of a personality torn between powerful biophysical instincts (or psychic urges) and what remained of his religious beliefs in gods or God. This is still the human situation today, except in relatively rare instances.

Idealizations, rationalizations, and transcendent justifications belong to the realm of "myths"; and myths are essential to the development of human consciousness, just as utopias are indispensable factors in the growth of man's social consciousness. Mankind can only become what a few visionary individuals have been able to envision, what they presented as fascinating ideals pervaded with charisma, and perhaps at least in some cases, what these men's lives actually demonstrated to be possible in the "here and now."

It is in the light of the preceding statements that we have to reconsider much of what astrophysics presents to us as facts. They are facts in terms of our belief in the physicality of the star-realm; but facts only relative to the type of outer events our limited material senses can perceive directly or with our instruments' help. Because man has an inherent need for order as a basis for a sense of security, our minds, obsessed with the concept of physical materiality and eager to make entities out of what he observes, build a cosmic type of order on the basis of cosmic "constants." The speed of light, the force of gravitation, the speed of some atomic processes, the red shift in the light-spectrum of distant star-systems,[5] are some of these constants. We believe in their constancy throughout universal space and at any conceivable time. Such a belief is certainly a "myth"; yet this does not mean, I repeat, that it is not "true" relatively to our present level of consciousness. It simply means that this belief represents an ideal which, at our present level of evolution, most human beings are compelled to accept as valid and necessary in order to feel secure. Any concept which upsets that belief menaces our sense of security—of universal "law and order"—and is at once called irrational and revolutionary.

Unfortunately for modern man's sense of security, the science in which our Western mentality placed its faith when the old medieval system of religiously revealed truths began to collapse, has now produced a picture of the universe which is increasingly upsetting because it seems to expand our world in an increasingly unimaginable way, in relation to both the nearly infinitely small and nearly infinitely large. Could it be that such near-infinitudes result from the fact that once we leave the realm of planetary materiality and solar centrality we can no longer significantly conceptualize our previously observed data in terms of the universal constants we still doggedly believe in? Could it be that, if we could operate at what I call the galactic level, we would not deal with infinitely vast distances in the space of physicality, because we would now be thinking and functioning in the space

[5] As the distance of a fast-moving object from an observer increases, the frequency of the sound or light vibrations emitted by that object appears to decrease. If we study the spectrum of the light of a star receding from us, we find that the characteristic lines of a few typical chemical elements (for instance, hydrogen)—in comparison to those of the light from a known laboratory source—are shifted toward the lower-frequency red end of the spectrum. This is what is called the red-shift. The faster the speed of the receding star, the farther it is from us.

of galacticity—and also in galactic time, the time of the greater Whole in which we merely are very small existential wholes?

"Could it be?" Of course this is a hypothesis; we cannot be sure, unless in some manner man's consciousness can emerge upon the plane of galactic being, or at least resonate to (or reflect) the type of consciousness associated with the kind of relatedness constituting galactic existence. If such a hypothesis can be made to act as a factor impelling us to proceed more consistently and securely on the Path, that, after many radical transformations, will lead us to the galactic level of consciousness, it becomes a myth. It exerts a fascination upon our minds. It compels our consciousness to expand from the sphere of physicality to the four-dimensional space of galacticity, from planetary darkness to stellar radiancy of light.

It is a myth, just as man's belief in gods—or in God—is a myth; yet this myth has been and remains indispensable because it has been driving human beings to an often heroic transcendence of their physical limitations and their Saturnian egos. In so doing, man has realized his essential nature as a human being. What I am trying to say in this book is that mankind today apparently needs such a galactic myth; and the popularity and extraordinary spread of astrology, even at its lowest level of validity, bears witness to the existence of such a need. If we understand what the need is; if we can truly meet it by a convincing analysis of what it is that man's consciousness must now transcend—the concepts of physicality, centrality, rationality, and egocentrically interpreted freedom and equality—then the facts revealed by astrophysicists may be so transfigured and transsubstantiated that out of them an inspiring picture of the Galaxy may gradually emerge. This picture, evoked by the image-making faculty of a few seers and "imagineers," [6] may inspire new generations to achieve a radical transformation of consciousness and of society.

[6] This word "imagineer"—a combination of "image" and "engineer"—was coined during World War II by a perceptive Californian newspaper writer, whose name I have forgotten.

.8.

Transpersonal Relationships
and the Galactic Community

It may prove impossible, on the basis of the physical means available to astronomers, to determine exactly what type of matter constitutes the bulging central part of our Galaxy. Vast "clouds" of hydrogen have nevertheless been detected there, and probably very little else. If we add to this the fact that hydrogen, and a lesser amount of helium, constitute nearly 99 per cent of the stuff of the universe that we are able to perceive— the remaining one per cent being divided among heavier atomic and chemical elements—a significant conclusion can be reached.

Hydrogen is the lightest element, its atoms being constituted by one proton and one electron; and whether we accept the Big Bang theory, the Steady State concept, or a combination of both, hydrogen is the first form of matter (in our sense of the term) to appear in the process of "creation." Helium is number 2 in the series of atomic elements, as its atoms are made up of two protons and two neutrons (forming their nuclei) and two electrons. In the plasma state of matter (the fourth state, after the solid, the liquid, and the gaseous) and under extremely high temperatures, hydrogen (number 1) becomes helium (number 2), and in the process an enormous amount of energy is released in the form of penetrating gamma rays and neutrinos—these mysterious subatomic "entities" which speed through the matter of solid planets as if it presented no obstacle.

We may therefore assert that at the beginning of our material universe hydrogen appears, emerging from some unknown and perhaps unknowable prematerial state, which we may simply identify as Space itself—or a higher dimension of space. Hydrogen may be formed all at once in a terrific explosion of protomatter—the *ylem* postulated by the cosmologist-physicist, George Gamow, interpreting the Big Bang theory advanced by Abbé Lemaître. Hydrogen may also emerge periodically from space, and the locus of such an emergence may be the central core of galaxies.

Whatever may be the case—and both theories may be reconcilable—the primordiality of hydrogen seems certain; and if the physical world can validly be said to represent a *reflection* of the spiritual reality of the cosmos, hydrogen by birthright should be considered the symbol of spirit at its source. The universal distribution of hydrogen parallels the all-pervasive and ubiquitous "presence," if not of the Supreme Spirit, at least of its manifestation in the realm of materiality.

On our Earth, two atoms of hydrogen combine with one of oxygen to form water (H_2O). Water is necessary for what we know as life; and in the atmosphere, oxygen (the 16th element) sustains vital processes. It is also involved in organic transformation and the life-death-life cycle. But if oxygen is essential to *life,* hydrogen is the base of operation of *spirit* whose activity in matter it symbolizes.

While such assertions are mythic rather than factually demonstrable, they find an occult corroboration in some statements made by H. P. Blavatsky in her great work *The Secret Doctrine* (original edition, Vol. II) written nearly a century ago:

Spiritual Fire alone makes of man a divine and perfect entity. Now' what is that "Spiritual Fire"? In alchemy it is HYDROGEN, in general; while in esoteric actuality it is the emanation of the Ray which proceeds from its noumenon. . . . Hydrogen is gas only on our terrestrial plane. But even in chemistry, hydrogen would be the only existing form of matter, in our sense of the term (Cf. *Genesis of the Elements* by Prof. W. Crookes, p. 21), and is very nearly allied to *protyle*. . . . It is the father and generator, so to say, or rather the *Upadhi* (basis) of both AIR and WATER, and is fire, air and water in fact—one under three aspects, hence the chemical and alchemical trinity. In the world of manifestation or matter, it is the objective symbol and the material emanation from the subjective and purely spiritual entitative Being in the region of noumena. Well might Godfrey Higgins have compared Hydrogen to, and even identified it with, the TO ON, the "One" of the Greeks. [p. 105.]

That to which Hydrogen is to the elements and gases on the objective plane, its noumenon is in the world of mental or subjective phenomena; since its trinitarian latent nature is mirrored in its three active emanations from the higher principles in man, namely, "Spirit, Soul and Mind." [p. 112.]

Three essential facts should be stressed: (1) hydrogen is the first material element to be formed; (2) its presence is detectable everywhere as a dominant factor; and (3) all we know about the central nucleus of our Galaxy is that it contains an enormously large amount of diffused hydrogen, possibly at the exclusion or near-exclusion of other atomic elements. It is indeed conceivable that the galactic core is like a cosmic fountainhead from which hydrogen is constantly emerging, or at least has emerged in the past. We do not know the way in which this process operates, but recent astrophysical theories suggest that the core of the Galaxy may be thought of as a "white hole" marking the emergence of hydrogen from another universe existing perhaps in another dimension of space—while the newly discovered "black holes" refer to the disappearance of the final forms taken by cosmic matter into mysterious whirlpools, sucked down by tremendous gravitational forces after the collapse of a star or a group of stars.

For occultists in various cultures of the past, the process of emergence of hydrogen on the physical plane is to be interpreted as the materialization (or physical plane manifestation) of a noumenal essence referring to a higher ("divine") level of being. Religions, mythologies, and metaphysical theories have variously described this process of concretization and "physicalization" of a transcendent spiritual reality. They have created a wealth of images adapted to the feelings and the mentality of the people of the corresponding epoch and culture. Today, as I have said, astronomy and the unparalleled spread of interest in astrology, offer us a new possibility of interpretation and symbolization, which provide us with a cosmic background for understanding the process of transformation we are witnessing at both the level of human consciousness and that of social and communal organization. Such a holistic background has antecedents in the occult concepts of the past, in that it implies the existence of a hierarchy of levels of existence and consciousness extending from the purest spirit to the densest matter, yet it avoids mythological personifications and abstrusely metaphysical intellectual arguments. It consists simply of an attempt to expand human conciousness from the level of physicality and totalitarian centralization of power in autocratic Suns to that of "galacticity."

What is involved in such an attempt is not only an expansion, but as well a *refocusing* of human consciousness and a basic *revaluation* of the social and psychological values which have long dominated the collective mentality of mankind. Such a process naturally arouses a great deal of resistance at all levels. By relating the new ideals to astrophysical concepts which appeal to the scientific mind and to which a great deal of publicity has been given, these ideals may be more easily visualized. The astrophysical omnipresence and primordiality of hydrogen—especially at the core of our Galaxy—become the symbol of a "corresponding" omnipresence and primordiality of spirit.

Symbols have enormous power. For instance, could one estimate the importance of what would take place in the collective consciousness of mankind if *everywhere* the picture of the Andromeda galaxy would replace that of the crucified Christ—or even of the cross—as a symbol of spiritual living? Yet to be spiritually valid such a substitution would *first of all* require a clear understanding of what I have called "galacticity." It would necessitate a *dephysicalization* of the universe beyond the boundaries of our planetary system. It would require a *practically applicable* understanding of what the concept of galacticity actually means as an ideal reorienting our everyday existence and our approach to interpersonal relationships—and therefore a realization of how it would transform our image of an ideal community.

A few paragraphs back I mentioned three basic facts emerging from recent astrophysical discoveries concerning the distribution of hydrogen throughout the cosmos. If we translate these facts into the language of galacticity in which spirit is symbolized by hydrogen, we have a picture of the universe in which spirit is the original substance of existence, and from this primordial substance everything else is derived. This "everything else" may only constitute one per cent of the cosmos; thus we are living in a universe which is essentially constituted by spirit. Spirit is "substantial"—which literally and etymologically means that spirit "stands under" every thing. It is particularly condensed, or it bubbles forth in sourcelike purity, at the center of galaxies. If there are other elements at these galactic cores, it is because space is filled with the immensely scattered remains of past universes—in whatever condition we may imagine these remains to be, perhaps as totally isolated atoms or particles, or as discords or statics in the great Harmony of Space, or as unconscious "memories" of failures (the *skandhas* of Buddhistic philosophy). Such disintegrated remains of a cosmic past, in the case of our Galaxy, have condensed to form the "dark clouds" which obscure for us the radiant fountainhead of spirit at the center.

Every star radiates what we perceive as light, as well as many other kinds of vibrations. Astrophysics has discovered that hydrogen is at the source of these radiations. If the recent concepts referring to the atomic reactions inside of the stars are correct—concepts which man has been able to apply to the production of hydrogen bombs—the brilliance of our Sun and the stars results from the release of energy produced by nuclear reactions in which hydrogen plays a preponderant role. The substantiality of spirit releases itself progressively in various modes of radiations. Light seems to be made of *particles* called photons; yet it acts also as *waves* because spirit—and all there is—can also be considered at a still more mysterious level of being as *vibrating Space.*

The concept of galacticity brings us only to a state of existence —what I have called the fourth dimension of space—whose main characteristic is INTERPENETRATION. We pass in consciousness from the third dimension, whose keynotes are physicality, centrality, and the condition of isolated and separative existence (or atomicity), to the fourth dimension, where there is no longer any separation. Where there is no separation, the possibility— in fact, the inevitability and necessity—of true community emerges. There can be no true community at the level of physicality and separateness. The experience of "I" is absorbed in community in the experience of "We"—the experience of interpenetration and all-inclusive mutuality.

When we can only think of such type of organization which the heliocentric system represents, the Sun is i-sol-ated in space and in lonely splendor, patriarchically controlling his group of planets. The Sun symbolizes then our equally lonely and proud "I am," which in its involvement in material concerns operates mostly as an ego—a jealous and possessive tribal spirit insisting that he is the one and only God. But when the Sun is seen and vividly understood as the star that it essentially is, it is known as a form of *universal spirit*—one form among billions of others. All these forms of spirit are "companions" within a vast galactic company of stars. It is not only a "company" (*cum-panis*: literally, "those who eat of the same bread") but a communion and community. All stars exist within a galaxy; they commune, as well as communicate, in waves of light. They are vibratory "forms of spirit," which together sound forth an evolving cosmic Chord—an immense motet in which a myriad of voices commune in interpenetrating relatedness.

Our Western society has produced conceptual and artistic musical forms ideally embodying such a principle of interpenetrating relatedness, and various attempts at community building have been made. Practically all of them have become disrupted by a combination of internal forces and external pressures, involving in some cases violent and total destruction. Destructive forces are inevitable whenever the attempt at community living is produced by physical-level and egocentric motives. In some cases organizations of a "heliocosmic" type are produced centered in one "solar" personage, who is the source of spiritual radiations; but true and lasting communities can be built only on the basis of galactic consciousness in which all "communicants" share.

This does not mean that the community has no center; but that center is not occupied by a massive super-Sun. The center is a fountainhead, a source *through* which spirit emerges; and all participants in the community share in that emergence. They are fed in common by the emerging hydrogen-spirit; and, in its primordial condition, that spirit is "no-thing," yet the potentiality of an immense number of "things."

At the galactic center infinite potentiality emerges as a source of actual existence. Existence is always finite; only the potentiality of existence can be considered infinite. Every galactic community has a finite purpose—a place and function in the universal Whole. But it is not a separative function. Galaxies form clusters of galaxies. Communities can only exist and prosper as communities if they realize and act out their relationship to other communities within the planetwide "Universal Community of Man."

In a galactic type of community, integration does not depend upon the existence of one all-powerful "solar" center compelling every participant to revolve worshipfully around it. Integration results from the complex interaction of beings, each of whom is a "star" in his or her own right and accepts his or her own place and function in the community. The binding power is that of love, in mutuality and understanding. The realization of unity is *evoked* in the constant and conscious interrelatedness of all the participants; wholeness rather than unity is the centralizing principle. This principle is a vivid but immaterial reality which has its shrine in the heart of every communicant. It may be felt as a unifying presence. It should be felt as a power evoked by the love of each for all; and that power has substantiality, inasmuch as it sustains and subtends the togetherness of all the participants who ritualistically commune in that substance. In astrophysical terms, this means that the gravitational force which keeps the galactic organization of stars integrated does not come from an immensely large super-Sun, but is rather the result of the interaction of the gravitational power of *all* the component stars. Group-cohesion is at work. The process is effective only if the relationship between all the units in the group is *transpersonal*.

This term *transpersonal* has two meanings, which unfortunately most people who use it do not understand. It may mean *beyond* the personality and its normal biopsychic urges and drives; but it can also mean *through* the personality, acting as a clear lens focusing at the level of physical activity, or at that of the mind and the feelings, a "downflow" of spirit. Typically, the devotee and the mystic seek to overcome the pull of biopsychic materiality and reach beyond to transcendent realizations; on the other hand, the Avatar—and usually in a less pure form, the creative genius and the great cultural hero—is a human being who more or less deliberately opens himself to a "descent" of spiritual power, releasing that power in socially or culturally fecundant activity.[1]

In the ideal galactic community, of which I have also spoken in various books and pamphlets as the "seed group," [2] transpersonal relationships should be considered not only as transcending the passional and egocentric pull of instincts and emotional possessiveness, but also as focusing the emerging power of spirit upon certain functional activities. This is a very important point, for the focusing process in a great many cases implies the joint dedication, either of two persons (perhaps, but not necessarily, of different sexes) or of a very small group of especially related individuals—a dedication to a particular function in the community. This means that the central and fundamental emergence of creative spirit and the outer flow of inspiration (or rather "in-spiriting") does not only operate in and through individuals; it can have effective overtones in individualized situations.

At the core of every star-being in the galactic community is a fully activated or latent *center of resonance* to the spirit which animates the whole. This center actually is the true Self; and we may imagine a "fifth dimension" of consciousness in which all these star-centers are not only in a state of constant interrelationship, but are in essence identical. This is the realization which the Hindu yogi tries to convey when, speaking to a disciple, he says: "I am thou." It is the realization of the metaphysical identity of the Supreme Spirit and of the individualized spirit inherent, but in most cases only latent in every human being.

Unfortunately, at the level of existence at which most human beings are conscious during this historical period, such an identification in a great many instances has dangerous, or at least confusing, results. It is very easy and tempting for a temporarily illumined person to allow what may have only been a brief

<hr/>

[1] Cf. Dane Rudhyar, *Occult Preparation for a New Age*, Part 3.
[2] Cf. *We Can Begin Again—Together* (Tucson, Ariz.: Omen Press, 1974), the chapter "Commune and Seed Groups."

experience of perfect attunement to the downflow of power from the central Source of spirit to sink to the level of physical existence. What was a galactic realization of spirit is unconsciously physicalized into a "three-dimensional" feeling of being a Sun to a group of planets, rather than a star that for a moment had resonated to a "four-dimensional" call for activity within a galactic community. As this occurs, "solar" pride and spiritual intoxication with transcendent power adulterate the memory of the experience and give it an ambiguous character. Seemingly valid results may be obtained as other individuals are drawn to the stimulation which the new "Sun" provides for them; but in the end this may lead to spiritual bondage, not only for the devotees attracted to such a heliocosmic type of group, but also for the individual who had proclaimed himself a Sun.

As an individual begins to experience his attunement to the spirit, he has always to face a crucial choice: to be a Sun, while *dreaming* of identification with the Supreme Spirit or, as a star among companion stars, to dedicate to the whole community whatever spiritual inflow has sought in him a focal point and channel for expression. To any sincere and spiritually honest individual, life brings the testing situation in which the choice has to be made; and the more evolved and spiritually dedicated the consciousness, the subtler and more difficult the test.

There are three fundamental kinds of test, or rather three levels at which the decision has to be made during the process of spiritual transformation of the individual. And these three levels can be referred to the specific character of the trans-Saturnian planets, Uranus, Neptune, and Pluto. In a subtle sense, they may be seen to correspond to the three "temptations" of Jesus in the wilderness (Matt. 4), if these temptations are understood in their most essential character.

In the first temptation, Satan suggests to Jesus, emerging from a forty-day fast, that he command the stones to turn into bread. What Satan seems to appeal to is the powerful instinct to satisfy physical hunger; but the individual starting on the Path of transformation is seized by another kind of hunger—the hunger for spiritual experiences that would not only feed his soul, but justify his having given up all that his ego cherished. Driven by Uranian restlessness and by the promise of an exalted state of consciousness implied in what the Uranian lightning has revealed in a brief—oh, so brief—flash of insight into the transcendent beyond, the "disciple on the Path" yearns for more, always more experiences—more spiritual food.

In the second temptation, the Devil suggests to Jesus that he prove his divine Sonship by throwing himself into a precipice, because if he does so, angels would surround him and carry him safely to the lower region where people would be able to see the miracle. This is the Neptunian test; for what is tested is the individual's use of normally invisible or "occult" powers to prevent him to fail as he comes down to meet those he is to teach and inspire. Will he use the glamour of spiritual power and prestige—a glamour related to Neptune—to impress those who are eager to believe in everything that seems to them miraculous; or will he bring them that water of the spirit, drinking which they will no longer thirst, and the vision of a "galactic" reality?

In the third temptation, Satan appeals to whatever form the ego may still have in the man who has attempted to leave irrevocably behind him the realm of Jupiter and Saturn—the realm where social power, glory, fame, and worship are the most basic allurements. The aspirant to rebirth in spirit must surrender all desire for power *over* other human beings. He cannot become a safe and valuable member of a galactic type of community if there exists in him the slightest desire, deeply unconscious as it may be, for acting as a Sun to a group of dark planets. This is the Plutonian test of total denudation—or, as the Christian mystic states, of absolute humility. Only if the Plutonian catharsis is successfully met can an individual be trusted to be a true "companion."

One can think of many other tests, but the three which are

mentioned in the Christ *mythos* are deeply significant. The hunger for spiritual experiences, the desire for display of miraculous powers surrounding one with transcendent glamour, and the deep yearning for self-glorification and power over other human beings—even if it be the subtle power that a healer may feel over those he has generously and effectively healed: these constitute three deeply rooted attachments which must be overcome and totally eradicated before the consciousness can be stabilized at the level of galactic being.

What forms reality and one's activity may actually take at the galactic level must remain a vast unknown until all the conditions for emergence are satisfied. They are not conditions arbitrarily imposed by anyone or any group; they refer to the kind of order and structural organization operating at the galactic level. Every level of existence has its own rhythm, its "laws of nature," its requirements for existence. As man aspires to operate at a level higher than that of physicality and of a solar type of dominant centrality, he has to adapt his consciousness and the workings of his mind—mind being consciousness in a definitely structured state of activity—to unfamiliar conditions produced by a transcendent, but just as "real" type of order. While he is gradually coming to understand what the new principles of organization are, and first of all in most cases to experience perhaps drastically what they are *not,* he lives in a state of transition. He performs, half-intentionally—and often unconsciously, and not without resistance and confusion—a "rite of passage."

Treading the occult Path is performing a rite of passage. Attempting to cross the sound barrier in a fast-moving plane or to overcome the earth-pull of gravitation is also such a performance, though it refers more to an intellectual and collectively oriented than to a vital and basic achievement. Earth gravitation for human beings born in the biosphere symbolizes the sum total of attachments and allegiances binding us to the type of society in which the ego is proud master or resentful servant, if not slave. But the individual encapsuled in protective machinery and in constant contact with his society does not accomplish a real passage in terms of transformation of consciousness, even if he experiences brief moments of illumination. These, alas, fail to last after he is caught back into the biospheric and social rhythms which he never actually allowed to fade out completely from his individual psyche.

On the true rites of passage, Uranus, Neptune, and Pluto are the only guides; but they do not work through or within machines. They act within the total person—or, as today in a collective sense, in the very substance of social progress. These in turn react upon the biological and biospheric conditioning of life in all its forms everywhere on the globe.

Uranus, Neptune, and Pluto are masked hierophants whose countenance and magnetism both attract and frighten. They inspire individuals to change; they provide fleeting visions of an imprecise goal; they may even frighten into life-or-death situations. They hit all the weak points in the mind's armor with uncanny precision. Bruised and seemingly defeated by his own intellectual or emotional blindness, the individual could easily collapse, if only of sheer exhaustion, if he did not hold vibrant in his heart the symbolic vision of the future community. Behind them, through them, the sky may become alive and singing the divine motet of galactic harmony. For our inexperienced ears, the tones may sound discordant, for they interpenetrate in a manner that scorns the safe patterns of ancestral kinship and cultural tonality. But to him whose ears are unencumbered by the heavy wax of biological entropy, the vast chording of stellar differences transsubstantiates itself into an ecstasy of unified lights. He finds himself surrounded by "globular clusters" of radiant light-sources that are many, yet one. He may, like Dante, behold the vast celestial Rose in whose throbbing core spurts of hydrogen-spirit are promises of new worlds.

·9·

The Challenge of Galacticity
in Humanistic Astrology

The exalting myth should become a practical inspiration to greater living in the midst of present-day conditions. How can the astrologer into whose heart and mind clients pour their insecurity, their hopes, their fears, their complexes, and their torments give them a fresh, creative, and rehabilitating understanding of their past, a more dynamic approach to present crises or uncertainties, and an inner feeling of what they can accomplish if they dare face the challenge of the transformative spirit?

This is what any truly "humanistic" astrologer who takes his work to heart would eagerly like to know. But the answer to the question as above stated cannot be formulated in general terms. Spirit acts in a focal manner only in particularly defined cases, leaving to the mind the task of generalizing and symbolizing the "as-yet-unknown" in images and myths. Yet how could the next step in any situation be revealed to an eager enquirer except in the form of symbols?

Any life situation, with its personal problems, of course is the outcome of a unique set of circumstances, antecedents, and future possibilities. But it may also be understood as a single variation on one of relatively few themes. These themes are the archetypes. Man, as member of a particular culture, sees them in a special light. The quality of that light—the character of human understanding—changes as the consciousness of the collective "culture-whole," and of the individual person born in such a sociocultural field of activity, unfolds and actualizes more of the cosmic potentialities inherent in archetypal Man.

When human consciousness passes from the condition of heliocosmic centrality and materiality to that of galacticity, it inevitably is beset by a multitude of problems of intellectual and emotional readjustment. In attempting to solve these problems, individuals follow many paths of psychological enquiry. Each path follows a specific line replete with conscious and unconscious symbolism. How could this be different, in view of the often unrecognized fact that each path is based on undemonstrable premises or paradigms? Some of these, enforced by the socioeducational system, are taken for granted; but others result from a more or less intentional repudiation of what had been learned in childhood or through joining a special group.

In America today, a person seeking help from the usual psychoanalyst or psychiatrist implicitly accepts—whether he is aware of the fact or not—the paradigms of his particular variety of Western society. If he consults the typical self-advertising astrologer, an *extracultural* line of approach will be followed which represents an ambiguous combination of conscious and semiconscious attitudes. The *countercultural* approach of most humanistic astrologers is conditioned by a somewhat unclear form of protest against, and escape from, the premises enforced by the institutionalized mentality of our present society. This becomes *transcultural* if the enquirer intuitively feels that he is living in a state of transition between two cultures—one of them slowly becoming obsolete, and the other in an as yet prenatal condition—and that he must take a positive, creative, and transforming stand in terms of such a situation. He unavoidably has to use

words, syntax, and data produced by the present-day group-con-
sciousness and its instrumentalities, most of which are the products of past concepts and attitudes; yet he can see through them
and reinterpret them in terms of a new vision.

The galactic approach, which it is this book's purpose only
to evoke, for to define it precisely today would be an impossi-
bility, should be called "transcultural" rather than "countercultural." Our present knowledge of the Galaxy is far too hazy and
incomplete to serve as a solid and truly consistent foundation
for a definitely "galactic" type of astrological approach. Nevertheless, if we have been stirred by an emergent intuitive feeling
that mankind is now evolving toward a new and as yet unclearly
formulated condition of individual and social consciousness, we
can use the radically transformed astronomical picture to symbolize that state of consciousness and being to which we aspire;
and by so doing we can experience our attunement to cosmic
reality and galactic rhythms in a way that will transcend not
merely the individualistically anthropocentric attitude of our official Euro-American culture, but the childlike devotional approach of archaic man.

Until the new model of the universe is more definite and
structurally sound, such an attunement has to remain intuitive
and largely a feeling-experience, except in the rare instance when
a visionary mind operates; but we know enough today to see
emerging a few basic facts that can be transmuted into great
symbols pointing to new life realizations. The problem facing
the future-oriented astrologer is how to use these symbols in an
interpretation of birth charts that would reveal the manner in
which the new level of reality and consciousness may affect the
psychological and spiritual development of the individual he or
she is attempting to guide on his or her path to self-transformation.

In attempting to solve such a problem it is first of all necessary
to realize that the classical type of astrology is an ambiguous
combination in which the archaic intuitions (and the terms char-

acterizing vitalistic religions) mix with the materialistic and mechanistic concepts of the Copernican period of our Western society. The most basic ambiguity refers, of course, to the two concepts of zodiac: the sidereal zodiac of *constellations of stars* and the tropical zodiac of *signs* representing twelve sections of the Earth's orbit. Another kind of ambiguity results from considering the Sun and the Moon both from the archaic point of view which sees them as the two Lights and, in modern astrological practice, as "planets"—even though popular "Sun-sign astrology" gives an overwhelming importance to the Sun. A third kind of ambiguity resides in speaking of "fixed" stars— an appellation which is not even truly consistent with the archaic picture of the sky, for in that picture every celestial light-body was moving; the only thing "fixed" being the patterns made by the stars as the whole sky moves in a combination of daily and annual cycles.

When an astrologer speaks of a conjunction between a star and a planet, he or she thinks only of their zodiacal *longitude*. But many stars have a very high celestial *latitude* while planets, which always move within the narrow band of the zodiac, have low latitudes. This difference in latitude takes away the meaning of the conjunction (or opposition). The usual practice therefore negates the three-dimensionality of the universe. In an astrology depending so exclusively on the zodiacal plane for its measurements and its symbols it is also unsound to speak of "midpoints." For instance, Antares, the great red star in the constellation Scorpio (but now at about Sagittarius 9°23′ in the tropical zodiac, thus at celestial longitude 249°23′), has a celestial south latitude of about 4½ degrees, while Sirius, the most brilliant star (longitude 103°43′, or Cancer 13°43′) has a south latitude of about 39½ degrees. The distance in longitude between the two stars is therefore 145°42′ and their midpoint would be at Virgo 26°34′. But speaking of such a midpoint would be ignoring the 35-degree difference in their latitudes; it would mean compressing the southern celestial hemisphere into a flat pancake represented by the tropical zodiac—a narrow band extending only a few degrees on either side of the ecliptic.

On the other hand, if we consider the stars Regulus (29°27′ Leo and 0½ north latitude), Spica (23°28′ Libra and 2° south latitude), and Antares (Sagittarius 9°23′ and 4½° south latitude), these three are just as close to the plane of the ecliptic as planets; thus, the two sets of celestial bodies can legitimately be related to each other; and their midpoints could be considered significant. The midpoints between Regulus and Spica falls at Virgo 27°01′. Interestingly, it has nearly the same position as the (to my mind illogical) midpoint between Sirius and Antares. The midpoint between Spica and Antares would fall at longitude 226°28′ or Scorpio 16°26′.

We cannot orient ourselves significantly in such a welter of uncertainties and ambiguities if we pay too much attention to the fragmentary and often contradictory information derived from a painstaking study of old records left by societies whose paradigms and basic feeling-responses we do not share. Most of these piecemeal records, in fact, came from the period of transition between the Archaic and the Classical eras, thus from the sixth to the first centuries B.C.—a period just as confused as the present one. Astrology for the individual at the very earliest began in the fourth or possibly fifth century B.C. The art of horoscopy, developed in Greece, Egypt, Rome, and later on in the classical sixteenth to eighteenth centuries at the courts of the aristocracy or for political and military purposes, represents only a transitional way of using celestial data in dealing with personal situations and events, a way adapted to a period that emphasized and eventually came to glorify the ego and its wants. The use of the zodiac in horoscopy should be related to the historical period that saw the rise of the Sun to a position of unchallenged importance and centrality, a rise which, at least as far as the Mediterranean regions are concerned, had its most dramatic manifestation in the short-lived worship of Aton, the Sun-disc, by the Pharaoh Akhnaton.

The realization that the universe is a "living" whole should not be confused with the worship of a central figure or symbol that dominates the world. In the purest and most metaphysical form of Vitalism, Space (capitalized) symbolizes the divine creative energy-substance from which everything is derived. Space finds in the stars focal points or lenses *through* which it exteriorizes its potential of existence, and constellations represent divine creative hierarchies, each of which constitutes a particular cosmic quality or principle. During the day, the Sun blots them out, because it brings to an all-powerful, highly centralized focus the creative life energy of the particular constellation in front of which it passes during a month of our earthly year. The Sun simply channels the cosmic power of one of twelve basic aspects of divine Space represented by the zodiacal constellations. These aspects of the cosmic energy of Space are *needed* by man and all living organisms on our planet in order effectively to actualize their potential of existence.

According to this vitalistic concept (or myth) the other constellations, sufficiently above or below the plane of the Earth's orbit so as not to be "zodiacal," are also immense sources of cosmic power, but mankind cannot *normally* use the energies emanated by these extrazodiacal constellations. Still, the larger stars in those constellations beam upon the Earth some of their power, and human beings who somehow can respond—and whose "fate" it is to respond—to these extraordinary powers may become "possessed" by them. This can lead either to spectacular success and fame, or to equally striking failures, downfall, or unusual illnesses. Medieval astrologers retained enough of these archaic vitalistic ideas to attribute to the most brilliant "fixed stars" the capacity to bring about abnormal or supernormal conditions in the lives of the persons in whose birth chart they conjoined Sun, Moon, and any one of the four Angles, especially the Ascendant and Mid-Heaven.

Any celestial phenomenon whose recurrence did not seem to fit into any known and understandable patterns of order (comets, for instance) was inevitably given a more or less "ominous" significance. Today, our awareness of cosmic order has acquired a new quality and has been greatly extended. As the character of what we understand by cosmic order is altered, so should the quality and level of our astrological interpretations. *Galacticity* refers to a newly envisioned type of order which recent astronomical discoveries evoke, though they are unable as yet to define it.

While astronomy seeks to establish the existence of order in celestial phenomena, astrology's function is to transform this observed order into a "myth"—that is, into a series of consistently interrelated symbols able to give a vivid and experienceable direction to the slow and always uncertain progress of individuals and societies toward an ever fuller actualization of the potential inherent in Man as an archetypal reality. The zodiac, with all the immensely ramified and diverse interpretation of its twelve signs, is a myth. *In its present form,* it presumably is the legacy of a group of wise men forming some kind of "Occult Brotherhood" or of priests who eventually become known as "Chaldeans," and in some instances "Sabaeans," though we cannot be at all sure how these names originated or what group of men these terms first designated. According to the *Encyclopaedia Britannica* ("History of Astrology") astrological concepts reached the Greek world "through a Babylonian sage, Berosus, who founded a school about 640 B.C. in the island of Cos and perhaps counted Thales of Miletus (639–548) among his pupils." But what remains of Berosus' writings is now generally called "apocryphal" and what he claimed to have been records of an immense antiquity are discredited by modern historians, who insist on condensing the periods mentioned in many ancient books, whether of Babylonian or Indian origin, into a very few thousand years.

From the point of view I have taken, whenever "facts" are susceptible of so many contradictory and changing interpretations, it is best to think of *validity* rather than of *truth*. Whether the zodiac of twelve signs does or does not have an immense antiquity, *its use in a present form* is conditioned by classical concepts based upon the need to deal with situations created by more or less individualized human beings and their problems. These situations did not exist in the archaic past of at least our present mankind; and the possibility that they may be deeply modified by conditions that will exist in a "new age" has to be faced. The galactic approach to astrology, which I am suggesting, is an attempt to face this possibility by interpreting in a creative spirit the new discoveries of astronomy.

The zodiacal concept should therefore be reinterpreted, even if at present for practical reasons, the astrologer cannot dispense with it. It is a basic frame of reference; but as I pointed out in the first part of my book *The Astrological Houses,* it would lose much of its importance in a truly "person-centered" type of astrology in which three-dimensional "birth globe" would replace our present two-dimensional birth charts. Here again a careful distinction between what we rather ambiguously call today the zodiac and a general division of any cycle into twelve phases, each of which has a characteristic meaning, is imperative.

When the "esoteric astrologer" sees in the zodiac a mythic picture of the descent of "the Soul" into matter and its reascent toward its original spiritual state, what he does is to use the annual, celestial journey of the apparently moving Sun as a symbolic drama in which the Sun is represented by the Soul. Yet what he symbolizes or celestializes is in fact the seasonal cycle of vegetation in temperate north-hemispheric regions—thus the process of life in the biosphere. This is logical and significant in societies based on agriculture and cattle raising, but this myth loses most of its relevance when applied to the problems of a modern egocentric individual whose personal experiences have very little to do with the seasons. Still this radical change in the basic life pattern of human beings does not take anything away from the archetypal meaning of a twelvefold division of a cycle and of the space around a man standing on the surface of the Earth, or of the geometrical solid, the dodecahedron, whose cosmic significance was stressed by Pythagoras and Plato.

Such a twelvefold scheme can be applied to a revitalized concept of astrological Houses, when the individual is seen actually standing at the center of a three-dimensional mandala, his "birth globe." It could be used in galactic astrology, if we knew enough about the structure of the whole Galaxy—which unfortunately we do not. We do not even know whether our solar system is part of a subgalactic system and whether our Sun revolves around a larger star or participates in a subgalactic community in which the principle of galacticity, rather than that of solar centrality, operates.

Because of our ignorance, people may say that the very concept of galacticity is premature. But so are all social utopias and philosophical-ethical dreams! They announce and attempt to formulate in broad terms what sooner or later must come. By imprinting the ideal upon the consciousness of human beings and small groups or communities, these dreams make possible the seemingly impossible. They gradually permeate and transform the personal practices, feelings, and behavior of an increasing number of individuals who have been moved by the vision. At the very least, they raise basic questions; and the ability, and the courage, to ask questions that go to the root of concepts and challenge generally accepted paradigms are essential factors in human evolution.

One can only move step by step. To speak of "humanistic" astrology was one step. To go from the humanistic to the "transpersonal" concept founded upon the principle of galacticity is a further step. It is a step to be taken by the astrologer as a human being, rather than a memorizer of textbooks featuring either old procedures or new techniques whose importance is claimed to be demonstrated by statistics of questionable validity. It is not so much what we can find in and add to an astrological chart that matters, but rather how we look at the chart and what our conception is of man and man's destiny or purpose in the universe—

and how we can significantly formulate it in terms that will inspire the client.

Nevertheless, the interested "reader" undoubtedly will still ask how he or she can actually apply the concepts this book features in his or her interpretation of personal charts, and whether the "fixed stars" should be given more importance than is usually attributed to them. To these questions I can only make tentative answers, the best that, at this time, I can formulate.

The fact that at present most astrologers refer to the Sun and the Moon as "planets" is already an indication of a break, confused though it be, with a strictly heliocentric approach. Neither can it be considered a return to the archaic approach. It implies that the astrologer thinks of the ten planets (Sun and Moon included) as symbols of ten basic *functions* operating in any organized system of interrelated and interdependent activities. This is the humanistic astrologer's approach—a holistic approach. An "organic" interpretation is established between all the factors marked on a circular birth chart, and the latter represents a mandala at the center of which the individual "I" stands as an integrative principle. There is nothing wrong in that picture, as it effectively symbolizes the present human situation. All that a consideration of the potentiality of "galactization" of human consciousness *adds* to that picture is a new and repolarized interpretation of the meaning to be attributed to (1) the Sun; (2) the trans-Saturnian planets, Uranus, Neptune, and Pluto; and (3) the stars.

(1) According to our galactic interpretation, the Sun should be given a twofold meaning. As a Sun, center of a system of planets, it is the source of the basic life energy. I have often spoken of it as symbolizing the particular kind of fuel on which the engine of personality runs—there being at least twelve such kinds of fuel, each represented by the Sun's position in a zodiacal sign, and therefore by the special kind of relationship between the Earth and the Sun at birth.

On the other hand, the Sun considered as a star—one among billions within the Galaxy—symbolizes the characteristic set of possibilities of consciousness and outer activity defining the human kingdom, and the archetype Man. Thus the actual physical relationship of the Earth to the Sun at the moment of birth of a human being symbolically indicates the manner in which this particular newborn organism is attuned to *one particular aspect* of the entire potential inherent in Man, and reflectively and bio-psychically in "human nature." If we were to mention only twelve such aspects of human nature, we would obviously speak in too general terms—which is why the popular Sun-sign astrology has so little validity, especially as it studies only the Sun's position in the zodiac. A finer kind of analysis is required which refers to a more individualized level of human values. The symbols of the 360 degrees of the zodiac, theoretically refer to such a level. I have discussed these symbols and their meaning in my book *An Astrological Mandala.* The "Sabian" set of symbols which I have reinterpreted may not constitute a final statement concerning the significance of the zodiacal degrees, but at present it is the most significant available—significant not only by its contents, but as well in view of the extraordinary manner in which it was obtained (cf. Part 1, Chap. 2: "The Sabian Symbols: Their Origin and Internal Structures").

The symbol of the zodiacal degree on which a person's natal Sun is located gives some indication—ambiguous though it be in many instances—concerning the particular aspect of human nature an individual person would develop if he or she fulfilled his or her innate human potential in tune with the vast overall pattern of the Galaxy in whose activities the Sun participates. In simpler terms, the degree position of the natal Sun refers to the essential purpose of the individual's life, provided one understands the word "purpose" in a sense that transcends the social category of culturally determined purpose.

For the sake of illustration I shall take the birth chart of the great German occultist and philosopher, Rudolph Steiner, a man of many philosophical, occult, educational, and artistic talents, a clairvoyant and the founder of the Anthroposophy Movement. He was born with the Sun at Pisces 9°20′; and the 10th degree of Pisces carries the following symbol and interpretation:

> AN AVIATOR PURSUES HIS JOURNEY, FLYING THROUGH GROUND OBSCURING CLOUDS: Man's ability to develop powers and skills which, by transcending natural limitations, allows him to operate in mental-spiritual realms. . . . He does so as an individual in command of powerful energies, but also as heir to the industry of countless innovators and managers . . . the symbol evokes the achievement of *mastery*. [*An Astrological Mandala*, p. 274.]

Such a symbol is certainly befitting, though one should evidently not deduce from it that Steiner was a "Master"! He simply represented the flowering of a long cultural tradition, probably directly or indirectly related to the Rosicrucian Movement.[1]

Another example is provided by the birth chart of President Dwight Eisenhower who was born when the Sun was on the 22nd degree of Libra—and only 5 degrees away from Uranus. The interesting degree symbol, as in most cases, should not be interpreted literally, yet it points to a quality which it may have been Eisenhower's function to demonstrate in his very special life.

> A CHILD GIVING BIRDS A DRINK AT A FOUNTAIN: The concern of simple souls for the welfare and happiness of less evolved beings who thirst for life-renewal. . . . In this symbol, the connection between "child" and "birds" implies a spontaneous, naïve rapport at the spiritual level, a soul-touch at the level of pure feelings. . . . The keyword: *solicitude*.

In Albert Einstein's birth chart the Sun is located on the 24th degree of Pisces, thus symbolized by:

> ON A SMALL ISLAND SURROUNDED BY THE VAST EXPANSE OF THE SEA, PEOPLE ARE SEEN LIVING IN CLOSE INTERACTION—Keyword: *centralization*.

---

[1] His chart is printed in my book *Person-Centered Astrology* (Lakemont, Ga.: CSA Press, 1972).

Whatever the symbol meant in Einstein's personal and spiritual life, it is interesting to note that his now officially accepted Theory of Relativity challenged the concept of spatial infinity and led to the picture of "island universes." He centralized many new discoveries and ideas into an integrative concept, and by this he presumably fulfilled his destiny of life purpose.

Very often the symbol not only has to be reinterpreted in relation to the particular life situation; but the individual may not be able to meet in a positive spiritual manner the archetypal task confronting him. The case of Benito Mussolini, the symbol of modern Fascism, is significant if we remember that his fascistic movement was born out of the fear of a newly spreading wave of Communism in Italy after World War I.

> A CONSERVATIVE, OLD-FASHIONED LADY IS CON-
> FRONTED BY A "HIPPIE" GIRL: This refers to a collective,
> cultural, and social crisis which challenges us to realize *the
> relativity of social values.*

In this quaint symbol we see a new ideal of existence challenging the old order. Mussolini chose to meet the confrontation by ruthlessly destroying whatever and whoever seemed to proclaim the need for the reform of an obsolete system.

(2) I have stated in previous chapters that Uranus, Neptune, and Pluto, while they are *in* the solar system, are not *of* it. They represent a three-pronged attempt to lead man's consciousness from a Sun-Saturn, three-dimensional state of relative bondage to the four-dimensional galactic level. I consider such an interpretation of the character and function of the trans-Saturnian planets essential, for it alone enables the astrologer to give a positive and transformative meaning—cathartic though it might be—to a multitude of outer events and inner confrontations which our society, and most psychiatrists and psychologists, are not able to evaluate in a constructive, spirit-oriented light.

Uranus, Neptune, and Pluto symbolize whatever in human life today can help both the majority of individuals, and the various cultures and socioreligious groups still demanding people's unquestioned allegiance, to accept the present crisis (and the impending new ones) as the only means for them of emerging into a wholesome and spiritually oriented state of existence. Even a psychotic episode, or, at the national level, a cataclysmic series of events (whether telluric or man-made) can become the means for radical transformation and spiritual rebirth. But this only happens if at least the main characteristic of the future condition is envisioned, thus becoming a consciously held and longed for ideal toward which man must strive. A profound lassitude and a disgust with present conditions are not sufficient, for these may only precipitate premature and aimlessly disruptive gestures that doom the revolt to futility.

There must be Uranian vision if Neptune and Pluto are to be fully accepted as hierophants leading us to the new life; and without the compassion and broad understanding of interpersonal relationship represented by Neptune, the type of activity symbolized by Pluto tends to be drastic and ruthless, even if intellectually and coldly justifiable under the prevailing conditions. Thus, the manner in which these three galactically polarized planets are related to one another—by *aspects,* by *"Parts"*, and/or by *midpoints* [2]—should be carefully studied; and this not merely in a strictly analytical manner but in terms of the holistic picture arising from their interrelationships. That picture has to be com-

---

[2] The astrological Parts—often called "Arabian"—are indices of the state of the relationship between two celestial bodies moving at different speed, when this relationship is referred to the Ascendant or to the other three Angles. The most-used Part is the Part of Fortune, relating the position of the Sun and the Moon to the Ascendant of a person's chart. It is calculated by adding the longitudes of the Moon to that of the Ascendant and subtracting from the sum the Sun's longitude. I have thoroughly discussed the Part in *The Lunation Cycle* (Berkeley, Ca.: Shambhala Publication). The Parts of Uranus to Neptune and Pluto, and of Neptune to Pluto, can be calculated in the same manner.

The midpoint between two planets simply represent, at least in theory, the zodiacal place at which their activities blend in a most focused manner. They are considered "sensitive points"; and obviously there are many of them, as in theory each pair of planets has two midpoints in opposition to each other.

pared with the one produced by the planets between Saturn and the Sun; the latter being studied in terms of the already-mentioned pairing of complementary planets (Jupiter-Saturn, Venus-Mars, Sun and Moon), and of the potentially transformative, if not cathartic relationships between Uranus and Saturn, Neptune and Jupiter, Pluto and Mars—and also in another sense Pluto and Mercury—two aspects of the mind.

Especially important in the first stage of the study of a birth chart are the transits of the trans-Saturnian planets over the Sun, the Moon, and the four Angles. These, and the age of the person whose chart is being studied, are matters for primary consideration, together with the age at which "progressed New Moons" [3] and Jupiter-Saturn conjunctions occur—and the natal Houses in which they take place. For instance, the House in which the last conjunction of Uranus and Pluto around Virgo 17° fell can give an important clue to the character taken by the urge for self-transformation (or collective reform and rebirth) in the life of the individual. If this individual was open to change, and consciously or unconsciously did not block a potential transformation, the House in which the conjunction occurred should tell *the most significant field* in which this process of partial metamorphosis, or at least of repolarization could have been focused. In the U.S. chart (with mid-Sagittarius rising [4]) this Uranus-Pluto conjunction fell in the ninth House, dealing with expansion, foreign adventure, diplomacy, philosophy, and religion—and 1965–66 were the years in which the Vietnam War became a crucial and transforming issue, and the use of psychedelic drugs polarized the Youth Movement. The conjunction occurred in the first House and close to the Ascendant of our ex-President who—

[3] For a study of the "progressed lunation cycle," see *The Lunation Cycle*, Chap. 7.

[4] Cf. my book *The Astrology of America's Destiny*. I stressed there the significant fact that Neptune crossed the Mid-Heaven of this U.S. chart when the atomic project was undertaken. Uranus made the same transit when Nixon was elected in 1968; Pluto was at the same degrees during the 1972 Presidential campaign; and Neptune will cross the United States natal Ascendant in 1976—our Bicentennial and another Presidential campaign.

for better or for worse—was then planning his 1968 electoral campaign.

The Houses in which the long sextile of Neptune and Pluto is taking place—and, in people born around 1900, the House in which the 1891–92 conjunction of these planets occurred—should also be carefully considered, *if* the individual is truly susceptible of responding to such a global call for reorientation and spiritual-mental rebirth. All such aspects—especially in most cases conjunctions, oppositions, and squares—refer to the *potentiality* of individual or collective experiences stimulating the process of transformation. In fact, every aspect, transits, or progressions in which the trans-Saturnian planets are involved may produce such a stimulation. In such cases, the astrologer whose consciousness is galactically oriented can intuitively sense the opportunities for transformation coming to himself or his clients; and bringing these openings to the consciousness *may* offset the usually strong, instinctual, resistance to change. It "may"; but, in many instances, this can also generate fear, if the possible change is seen as a *future* possibility and thus as a challenge one may not be as yet ready to meet at the time.

Astrology should not be considered a *predictive* science. The astrologer's task is to help the individual to understand the deeper, more objective, and transformative implications of what is taking place *at the time of the consultation*—or at most the nature of trends which have already been recognized by the client, but seem not to have been understood for what they could mean if faced in the spirit of spiritual growth.

The fundamental problem for the astrologer is, therefore, how to evaluate his client's ability to react constructively to what is mentioned to him as a possibility or trend upon which he should focus his attention. Extreme care is needed if unwholesome psychological reactions are to be avoided. The essential fact to bear in mind is that whatever Uranus, Neptune, and Pluto may seem separately to indicate—whether as concrete events or trends of personal development—these indications refer to *a threefold process* that should be seen as a complex whole. What is at stake is the manner in which a human being can best and most significantly travel on the Path of self-transformation. It is one Path, one process. It begins in the darkness of the jungles of this Earth— natural or man-made as these jungles may be—and it ends in the light-consciousness of which our Galaxy is the celestial symbol and factual representation.

(3) If we attempt to give a precise or episodic meaning to what classical astrologers called "fixed stars" we actually have very little on which to base a convincing judgment. A book like Vivian E. Robson's often-quoted *The Fixed Stars and Constellations in Astrology* (London, 1923) provides us with a collection of data from Hellenistic, medieval, or classical sources upon which it would be not only unwise, but often psychologically dangerous, to rely. Other books like the otherwise valuable *Encyclopedia of Astrology* by Nicholas de Vore (New York 1947), can be even more destructive in the interpretation of what the stars indicate when they conjunct the Sun, the Moon, and the natal Angles. Sooner or later some "scientific astrologer" will make an exhaustive statistical study of the stars' presumed influence, probably when near the Ascendant and/or the Mid-Heaven; this is likely to produce more problems and unfortunate results when the statistical data—which might be valuable in terms of *large groups*— are used to give advice to individual clients, statistics having no value when applied to individual cases.

Planets have meanings in the solar system because of their hierarchical rank—or, more simply their distances from the central Sun. They also acquire meaning because of their positions in the system relative to us, observers on the Earth—thus, geocentrically; Venus and Mercury being inside, and the others outside, the Earth's orbit. These meanings are archetypal and fundamental; from them a great variety of secondary, tertiary, etc. characteristics can be deduced, referring to superficial features and personal reactions. Unfortunately, as I have already stressed, the interior structure of the Galaxy is mostly unknown. Our traditional knowledge of stars has been geocentric; men noticed their brilliance or their faintness, the geometrical designs (constellations) they formed in the sky. Today, by complex observations and calculations, astronomers are able to deduce their "absolute" luminosity and their relative distances; but we are left with a vast amount of uncertainty. If there is a subgalactic system to which our Sun belongs together with the most brilliant stars we perceive, we do not know its structural organization inside of a space-field whose diameter may measure some 10,000 light-years.

As a star, the Sun evidently is involved in interactions among the stars of our Galaxy. This involvement operates in the galactic dimension of cosmic existence, just as the interrelationship between the planets of our system has meaning in terms of heliocosmic values. Mixing the two levels, galactic and heliocosmic, can only produce confusion, especially when we consider astrology a language in which symbols of different orders are used. On the other hand, we are compelled to accept the possibility that what occurs at the higher, more inclusive level of the galactic whole affects the conditions of existence of the lesser units within it. We should try to differentiate between star-to-star relationships— thus how our Sun as a star is directly affected by its relation to other galactic stars—and the general condition prevailing at any time within the entire field of the Galaxy.

In the first case we are dealing with changes occurring in our Sun, changes transmitted to the Earth's biosphere by solar rays and according to the state of the entire solar and interplanetary field of activity; while in the second case we are considering how anything on this Earth is affected by the overall state of galactic space, a space in which we exist, just as fishes live in the sea. This is similar to the way in which a factory worker is affected not only by the reaction of the owner-manager of the factory to laws and regulations passed by the State and to the policies of his friends or competitors, but by the overall "state of the nation" to which both he and his manager belong—i.e., by the general economic situation (the cost of what he has to buy) and the mores of his society.

In the language of astrological symbolism, the state of the galactic "nation" should be measured and interpreted by taking the galactic plane (also called galactic equator) as a fundamental plane of reference. This galactic plane is easily visualized, since our Galaxy has the shape of an elongated disc with a bulging core. In order to measure the position of stars in the Galaxy in relation to its equatorial plane, we need a starting point. Before 1961, this starting point was where the galactic equator crosses the celestial equator (an extension of the plane of the Earth's equator) in the constellation Aquila; but in 1961, astronomers decided to use a different point, and galactic longitude is now measured eastward from the center of the Galaxy in Sagittarius. One of the reasons for the change was to conform to the position of a ring of hydrogen radio radiation exactly at what is now galactic longitude 0°. Galactic latitude is measured north (positive) and south (negative) of the galactic equator. The four directions of the galactic plane are said to be toward the constellations Cygnus, Carina, Sagittarius, and Auriga, and our Sun is moving in the direction of Cygnus or Hercules, and away from Carina. Moving toward Auriga would be moving toward the rim of the Galaxy; moving toward Sagittarius, toward the galactic center. The Sun, I repeat, is far away from the galactic center, and located on the inner edge of the Orion arm of the Galaxy.

The basic question is: Should a modern astrologer attempting to think in galactic terms, retain the old strictly geocentric and empirical approach to the assumed "influence" of *single* stars, or is it possible for him to adopt a more holistic and truly galactic approach, interpreting the stars' characters in terms of their position in the Galaxy as well as of their nature and "age" as stars?

It seems evident that we lack sufficient knowledge to follow the second line of approach; we can nevertheless embody a certain amount of logical consistency in our attitude. As long as astrology is based upon what occurs in the sky close to and on either side of the plane of the ecliptic, only the conjunctions of the stars close to that plane (i.e., with low celestial latitude, north or south) with the planets of our solar system should be taken into consideration. In other terms, we should consider significant only the interactions between the stars and planets moving along the plane of our Earth's operation in the solar system, i.e., the zodiac. (That plane is close to the Invariable Plane of the solar system which, in terms of celestial mechanics, symbolizes the stability of the orbital relationship of the planets to the central Sun.) On the other hand, the galactic equatorial plane being inclined 62 degrees to the Earth's equatorial plane, is far from coinciding with the plane of the ecliptic; and this can logically be interpreted to mean that the *operative* relationship of the Sun to its planets is very different in orientation from its *companionate* relationship with its companion stars within the galactic Whole.

Because of Pluto's extremes of latitudes, we may allow to the zodiacal belt a width of 18 degrees of either side of the ecliptic. This enables many of the most brilliant stars to be included among those able to affect planets moving along the ecliptic. Betelgeuze, with southern latitude 16°2′ (present zodiacal longitude Gemini 28°23′), would still belong to this category, but not Sirius (latitude 39°36′–longitude Cancer 13°43′), nor Polaris, Wega, Fomalhaut, or the stars of the Great Bear. Algol, traditionally considered the most evil star of the sky, supposed to "cause misfortune, violence, decapitation, hanging, electrocution, and mob violence" (Robson, *The Fixed Stars*, p. 123), would not be included either. But, some of the often-mentioned stars, such as Alcyone (one of the Pleiades at longitude Taurus 29°), Aldebaran (Gemini 9°25′), Al Hecka (Gemini 24°24′), Tejat and Dirah (1st degree of Cancer), Wasat (Cancer 18°08′), North and South Asellus (early Leo), Regulus (Leo 29°17′), Spica (Libra 23°28′), Khambalia (Scorpio 6°34′), South Scale (Scorpio 14°42′), Antares (Sagittarius 9°23′) are found near the ecliptic.

If, however, we think of the possible effects which a star, located anywhere in the sky, might have, not on planets of our solar system, but on the consciousness and character of an *individual human being* living on the surface of our globe and facing his own sky, then, *any star to which that individual can relate,* consciously or unconsciously, may be worth considering and endowing with meaning. The problem of determining such a meaning remains extremely difficult, and our classical tradition may not be relevant to the state of consciousness and social behavior of a modern individual. One thing, however, seems certain, on the ground of logic and consistency. A star should be endowed with an "influence" only if it is found to rise (at the Ascendant), to culminate at the zenith, and to set in the West—and possibly if it is at the nadir, affecting the root of individual being. This influence should have nothing to do with the character of the zodiacal sign in which it would be placed if its position were reduced to celestial longitude. Neither should Ptolemy's practice of characterizing a star's influence in terms of the nature of two planets be considered valid in theory, even if it may possibly give a vague idea of what the influence might be, if it is felt at all.[5]

Such an influence need not be felt, and probably is not felt in an *individualized* manner if a person's mind is not sufficiently evolved to respond consciously to galactic *values*; yet an individual may become involved in a collective response, for instance as resident in a country or town, or as member of a persecuted race or religious organization—just as it is reasonable to suppose that the Sun, as a star, is affected at all times by the condition of the galactic field in which it moves. This effect is most likely transmitted to the entire solar system, in the form of radiations. These may influence the Earth's climate, producing drought or deluges, ice ages, and perhaps even earthquakes, which in turn may more or less crucially affect the lives of individuals.

I do not feel that our knowledge of such matters is reliable enough to warrant the type of pronouncements that fill astrological

[5] For more information concerning the traditional classical interpretation of the "fixed stars," see Appendix.

textbooks; and I must once more stress the fact that even scientifically reliable statistics would not indicate how a *particular
individual* can be expected to respond to the factor having been
statistically studied. If an astrological factor is constructive in 75
per cent of the cases, the individual client confronting the astrologer can always belong to the 25 per cent for whom it may have
a destructive or no effect at all. This may seem obvious to any
thinking person; yet it appears not to be, judging from the kind
of statements one constantly hears in astrological circles.

What—some puzzled readers may ask—is the value of astrology?
In my view, it is to help people meet and assess their experience
in terms of a more-than-subjective and more-than-personal frame
of reference—a holistic frame of reference in which every aspect of
the personality, and even life event or transforming experience,
finds *its most significant place and function as one particular
phase of the lifelong process of growth and actualization of innate potential.*

If I did not personally believe in the possibility for astrology
to provide this kind of help, I would have had nothing to do
with such a field of enquiry; and it could best be left to fortune-
tellers and entertainers. Predictions referring to the material systems constituted by a very large number of units studied by
physicists and chemists are valuable for increasing man's control
over a potentially inimical environment and in organizing everyday or even long-term behavior; but predictions relative to psychic-
mental and individualized human factors can be not only self-
fulfilling; in the long run they unavoidably tend to materialize
and mechanize our "image of man." The outer results at first may
appear impressive in material terms, yet the eventual outcome is
bound to be spiritually blightening. It can also be physically
destructive, and mankind today is compelled to face such a possibility.

This is the main issue, and not whether this or that kind of
technique, new or hallowed by its antiquity, is more or less pro-
ductive of results which can be nicely tabulated; that is, whether

or not "it works." Just as any national language "works" for the citizens of that nation, whose minds have been trained to think and communicate in terms of the set of symbols and vocal sounds of which the language is made, so any consistent and widely used astrological system and technique can work for the astrologers trained to use it regularly and intelligently. It works for them, because it is the system and technique best attuned to their mentality and to the mentality of the clients they attract.

In the same manner a Freudian psychologist normally attracts men and women for whose problems a Freudian analysis, at least at first, provides the best solution. The solution may produce new problems, which in turn may demand a Jungian or Transpersonal investigation, for man's consciousness is not static. Meeting a difficulty at one level may lead to the challenge of dealing with a higher or deeper level of awareness, and at this level a more meaningful set of disturbances or opportunities for growth may be revealed. The same thing is true with regard to an astrological approach. The popular Sun-sign astrology dispensed by newspaper columns and magazine articles may pave the way, however crudely and ineffectually, to a person's awareness of being "influenced" by extrapersonal and supersocial factors, and therefore of participating in the rhythm of the universe. It may be a naïve awareness, based on most general and—in the way they are formulated—even unsound concepts. But is it not what also happens with established religions, in which the statues of saints or the image of a bearded fatherly God sitting on a throne somewhere in Heaven are being offered for worship? Yet such naïve anthropomorphic practices can and do "work" for the person with a total unquestioning faith, and miracles do happen *for them*. The real question in such cases is not whether the miracles "actually" happen, but whether the happening produces lasting individual growth in consciousness, or leads to a deeper bondage to the level of consciousness which made the mysterious event possible. Statistics as to what percentage of very sick people making a pilgrimage to Lourdes in France are miraculously cured would have no meaning whatsoever, because it is not the physical facts that matter, but the human being's state of consciousness and his or her capacity to become more than he or she was at the start of the process.

Even if it seemed on the outside to be glorious, a strictly ordered civilization of human automatons would be the most tragic failure mankind could experience. Humanity is experiencing today severe and perhaps decisive planetwide crisis because it is dominated by our Western culture which failed to ask sufficiently basic questions, or rather that gave tragically benumbing materialistic answers to the fundamental ones: What is Man, and what is the meaning of Man's existence? The astrology now being practiced in America and Europe, whether at the fortune-telling or the statistical-scientific level, is the product of a collective mentality whose controlling rationalistic and egocentric patterns originated in ancient Greece and Alexandria, and further crystallized in Rome. The time has come when the classical concepts and procedures should be transformed in response to the emergence of a new spirituality able to repolarize completely and to expand the consciousness of constantly larger groups of human beings becoming aware of new levels of existence and new possibilities of growth as individuals.

It is to them that this book is dedicated. This book is certainly not a definitive statement. It is meant to be a call for reorientation and transcendence, an attempt to evoke as yet unenvisioned possibilities, a challenge to creative understanding. If it speaks of remote planets and far more distant stars, it is because astrology is today more than ever a convenient, because popular, means for the symbolization of man's ability to attune his consciousness and his life to the rhythms of ever-greater realms of existence. If we understand these rhythms and all the implications of a galactic dimension of consciousness in which all forms of existence interpenetrate in unceasing contribution to the supreme harmony of the cosmic Whole, we may then succeed in projecting this understanding upon that aspect of our minds whose work is to build new structures of individual and collective behavior; and mankind at last may emerge from the era of conflicts and frustrations, of hunger and pollution into the age of planetary harmony and plenitude of being.

Probably the most complete book on the "fixed stars" is Vivian E. Robson's *The Fixed Stars and Constellations in Astrology*. In his Preface, dated July 5, 1923, Robson mentions his indebtedness to a book by Alvidas (whose work, *The Fixed Stars*, is also now available) and to a quite fascinating large volume by Richard Hinckley Allen, first published in New York in 1899 and reprinted in 1936.

This last-mentioned book does not deal with traditional astrological interpretations, but instead studies the sources and many variations of the names of the stars, and their mythological associations and equivalents in non-Western cultures—especially Hindu and Chinese. The majority of the names actually came to Medieval Europe from the Arab astrologers; but the term "Arab" is probably misleading, for it may refer to people who lived in the regions where once Babylon flourished but had very little Arab blood. If one believes Arnold Toynbee's idea that Arabic culture mainly revived the once arrested "Syriac civilization," the Arab astrologers therefore inherited, if not literally, then psychically, the concern for the stars which, even since the days of Ancient Greece, have been associated with Chaldea. It may be that one would find more profit in studying this book and the mythic association of ideas implied in the stars' names, than in relying upon the characterization of a star's influence in terms of the nature of one or two planets to which the star is supposed to be related; for such an assumed relationship would connect two sets of entities which operate at two different levels (or dimensions) of existence. By making use of such "correspondences," one may miss what is really essential in the characterization.

Robson writes: "the fixed stars give strength and energy to the planets and modify their effects, but at the same time the nature of the planet exercises a strong controlling influence upon the result." He also asserts that "the influence of the fixed stars differ from that of the planets in being much more dramatic, sudden and violent . . . producing tremendous effects for short periods, and, after raising the natives to a great height, dropping them suddenly and bringing a series of dramatic and unexpected disasters. . . . It may be taken as a fairly well established rule that the stars do not operate alone, except perhaps in those cases where they are situated on angles, and therefore their chief effect is transmitted by the planets. They seem to form an underlying basis upon which the horoscope is built, and if a planet falls upon a star, its effect is greatly magnified, giving it a prominence in the life that is quite unwarranted by its mere position and aspect in the map." [pp. 92–93.] Ptolemy gave no rule for the determination of a star's nature in terms of one or two planets. If two planets are mentioned, the first one "is considered to represent the chief influence of the star. The second one denotes a kind of modifying influence."

Robson lists and studies one hundred and ten stars, listing them by their celestial longitude, and therefore by their position in the tropical zodiac. These positions gradually change because of the movement called the precession of the equinoxes, at the average rate of about 1 degree of longitude in seventy-two years. Here follows the names and assumed natures of some of the stars most often mentioned by modern astronomers. The positions of these stars are according to *The Astrological Annual Reference Book* (Symbols and Signs, Calif.) and are for the year 1972.

SIRIUS (Cancer 13°43′ – 39°36′ south latitude) This most brilliant of the stars is said to be of the nature of Jupiter and Mars. It is the Dog Star (constellation *Canis Majoris*) and it is assumed to predispose to dog bites, but otherwise to give Jupiterian honors, fame, wealth. According to Alice Bailey's *Esoteric Astrology*, Sirius has a most important relationship to our Sun of which it is, in a cosmic sense, the Higher Self. This may be the reason why when the Sun is conjunct Sirius in longitude, it sometimes bestows great power. This is the case in the United States' chart for July 4, 1776. Sirius has been called by H. P. Blavatsky (in *The Secret Doctrine*) "The Great Instructor of Mankind," and related to Mercury and Buddha or wisdom.

ALDEBARAN (Gemini 9°25′ – 5°29′ south latitude) A star of first magnitude, the left eye of the celestial Bull; for the ancient Persians, one of the four Watchers of the Heavens, of the nature of Mars according to Ptolemy, giving honor but also associated with violence and accidents.

ANTARES (Sagittarius 9°23′ – 4°34′ south latitude) A binary star in the heart of the celestial Scorpion; of the nature of Mars and Jupiter, suggesting honor, riches, but also violence, sickness, treachery, etc.

WEGA (Capricorn 14°56′ – 61°44′ north latitude) of the nature of Venus and Mercury. Though said to give beneficence, refinement, it also is believed to have a number of unpleasant characteristics. In some eleven thousand years it will become our Pole Star.

SPICA (Libra 23°28′ – 2°03′ south latitude) In the Virgo constellation this star is given a special importance by siderealist astrologers in determining the relationship between the zodiac of signs and that of constellations. It is said to have a benefic character, especially when near the Ascendant or the Mid-Heaven—and to be of the nature of Venus and Mars, or Venus and Jupiter.

RIGEL (Gemini 16°27′ – 31°08′ south latitude) A star of the nature of Jupiter and Mars, and BETELGEUZE (Gemini 28°23′ – 16°02′ south latitude) of the nature of Mars and Mercury, are first magnitude stars in Orion. It has long been my belief that Betelgeuze (from Arabic words meaning "the House of the Lord") is in some manner related to the impending Aquarian Age, while Regulus has been presiding over the Piscean Age which started, according to my calculations, soon after it entered the zodiacal sign, Leo. Regulus is passing now through the last degree of Leo, symbolized by the Sphinx, the entrance to the secret path leading to the Great Pyramid and, within it, the Chamber of Initiation. As Regulus leaves the sign, Leo, Betelgeuze will enter the solstitial sign, Cancer. The Aquarian Age will begin.

REGULUS (Leo 29°17′ – 0°28′ north latitude) of the nature of Mars and Jupiter. In various cultures this star was called King, Ruler, or Mighty. It represents the heart of the celestial Lion. Being very close to the ecliptic, it is almost covered by the Sun on the 21st of August. At much higher latitudes, the Lion's Tail star is DENEBOLA, said to be of the nature of Saturn and Venus; and bringing military power, honor, wealth, but also in the end failure or illness.

ALCYONE (Taurus 29°38′ – 4°02′ north latitude) Though a less brilliant star in the Pleiades, in olden days was believed to be the center of our universe. Occult writers give a great importance to the Pleiades, and relate this group of stars to Sirius, also to the stars of the Great Bear (cf. Alice Bailey's *Esoteric Astrology* p. 679 and elsewhere).

POLARIS (Gemini 28°11′ – 66°06′ north latitude) Our present Pole Star in the constellation Ursa Minor, is given the nature of Saturn and Venus. Next century, the Earth's polar axis will point to it as exactly as it ever can.

ARCTURUS (Libra 23°51′ – 30°46′ north latitude) was given the nature of Mars and Jupiter (like Antares) by Ptolemy, but Alvidas believed it should have been Venus and Mercury. It has been connected with Ursa Major, the Big Bear, and is one of the first stars mentioned in very old records.

ALTAIR (Aquarius 1°24′ – 29°19′ north latitude) The nature of this pale yellow star in the neck of the Eagle constellation has been characterized in different ways by different authors—Mars and Jupiter, Saturn and Mercury, even Uranus.

FOMALHAUT (Pisces 3°29′ – 21°08′ south latitude) This southern-sky star was also once of the four Royal Stars in ancient Persia, the Watcher of the South, marking then the winter solstice. Its nature is given as a combination of Venus and Mercury.

These characterizations, and the statements previously quoted from Vivian Robson, were written at a time when the nature, size, and structure of the Galaxy were not clearly understood. They may be valid at the classical level, and for the classical type of astrology which has been in use for centuries. For the astrologer who operates at that level, and who wishes to satisfy the expectations of clients conditioned by the popular concept of astrology as a predictive science—or at best as a means simply to analyze character—the traditional approach to the "fixed stars" may have some validity. Yet because in most cases, dramatic and spectacular characteristics are attributed to these stars, the knowledge of these characteristics can well increase, either already present fears or unwholesome expectations of great fame and fortune, in people fascinated by this branch of astrology. Thus any tendency toward paranoia may be given more power. The value of knowledge always depends on the ability of the knower at the time to use the data constructively; that is, on his or her ability to assimilate the knowledge and make it serve the purpose of fuller self-actualization. For this reason I repeat that an astrologer's most valuable asset is the capacity to feel intuitively his client's ability significantly and validly to use any information or interpretation being given. This capacity is particularly needed if what is told refers to spectacular events and, even more, if the astrologer suggests the possibility of a character or destiny transcending the range of expectations normal for the client, considering his age and the level of his culture.

EPILOGUE

What follows is an attempt to present as succinctly and clearly as possible the metaphysical concepts on which the picture of the universe and the Galaxy introduced in this book is founded. Some points, only barely touched upon here, are developed further in my book *The Planetarization of Consciousness*.

When we consider the type of centrality apparent in our solar system, we think of it in three-dimensional terms. A central mass of energy-substance rules over all the component parts of the system in two fundamental ways: it keeps the system integrated by its gravitational pull, but it also unceasingly radiates energy at various frequency levels. The central entity dominates the behavior of the system; it binds, yet it illumines and vivifies. It is the archetype of the beneficent autocrat, the divine Patriarch.

In the usual kind of mandala, the center of the figure is occupied by an entity to which everything in the mandala is related and toward which all more or less diverse, disparate, or conflicting parts of the whole geometrical figure converge. The mandala is used as a means of centering the consciousness, in whose mental field a vast variety of contents and fleeting shapes constantly move, often in a state of aimlessness or disarray. The ideal which all "great religions" seek to embody is the unification of all men living on this mandala globe, the Earth. In order to centralize this process of unification, the *theistic* religions stress the existence of God, a Supreme One. Because of the level of consciousness at which most of mankind has been operating, at least in recent millennia, this ideal of centrality most of the time has been "physicalized"; the One God has taken a physical appearance, usually in man's "image and likeness." He has also been worshipped as the Sun's disc, Aton; and occultists have spoken of it as the Central Sun or Spiritual Sun. Today, as the mandalalike shape of our Galaxy has become popularized, many hold the idea that a glorious super-Star might exist at the center of the Galaxy. Unfortunately (or perhaps fortunately) hidden from our human eyes by clouds of dust (which may symbolize man's karma-laden state of consciousness) this central super-Star might be the "Spiritual Sun" of Occult and mystical lore, around which all stars within our Galaxy would turn, as courtiers once moved in reverent awe around the throne of the Persian emperor, or of any "king by divine right."

There may be such a super-Star in the bulging core of our spiral Galaxy; but, according to the few available data and various intuitive realizations, there more likely is none. The center is not a particular mass of energy-substance of tremendous power and size, but rather a "white hole" through which energy-substance emerges, or has long ago emerged into the four-dimensional space of the galactic field—a fountainhead, not a huge ball of matter in the plasma state. What therefore keeps the Galaxy integrated as a cosmic whole is not the gravitation generated by an immensely massive center, but *the harmonic interplay of the gravitational pull of all galactic stars.* It is the holistic power of the galactic Community in which every star participates. And it participates in it because no star is separate from any other stars. They all interpenetrate. They constitute a true cosmic Community.

This does not mean, I repeat, that there is no central area. The principle of centrality is *implied* in the convergence of the gravitational forces of all the stars. It would also be implied in the periodical emergence of new energy-substance at the central fountainhead. At that place of power, a higher-dimension of existence—of which I have spoken as the fifth dimension of space—exerts a centrifugal force upon the four-dimensional space of the Galaxy, of which we see only a reflection in our three-dimensional consciousness of physicality. It is this reflection which some astronomers tentatively interpret as a "white hole" out of which new hydrogen (or protohydrogen) emerges. The "white hole" is polarized by the "black hole" into which old matter is irresistibly drawn by immensely powerful gravitational forces.

When I speak of a fourth dimension of space (which has nothing to do with the Einsteinian fourth dimension, time, used for the purpose of measurement), what is implied is the Principle of Relatedness; and Relatedness implies Form, whether at the physical or the mental level. The concept of a fifth dimension of space is founded upon the principle that a "will to be" has to be postulated at the root of all forms of existence. This can be expressed also by saying that an urge to become circle or sphere inheres in every mathematical point. It is an immensely powerful drive. It implies not only expansion, but creativity.

Creativity is one of the two aspects of cosmic Motion, and at this level of Space there is nothing but Motion, or Force in motion. It was symbolized in ancient India by the Great Breath. A *cosmogenic* act of creation—the exhalation of energy—is followed by a *catacosmic* process (inhalation), in which everything is being drawn back to the state of nearly dimensionless point. "White holes" and "black holes" constitute critical stages in these two processes. In China this dualism of Motion was represented by the Yang and Yin forces contained within a circle; the circle symbolizing the ineffable Tao, the ultimate reality of Space—which one might also call its sixth dimension.

With the fifth dimension, we reach a metacosmic state. It is a state of pure energy, however one may imagine it. There is, however, no point in trying to "imagine" it, because it transcends all spatial forms or images. Space at that level is in a condition of "metacosmic" union with Time, considered as infinite duration beyond all possibility of measuring. When the creative drive dominates (when Yang is more powerful than Yin), Time manifests and out of the "love" of Space and Time, a universe is born. During the cosmogenic half of the process Time, in terms of our kind of physical measuring, is flowing very slowly. As the cata-cosmic drive toward reabsorption into the point becomes the stronger urge (Yin dominance), Space contracts, and Time accelerates, and Consciousness expands. The "timeless" Now corresponds to the mathematical point. According to some astronomers the stars near the galactic center have greater speed than those in the distant arms of the Galaxy. As one comes close to the center of creativity, what we experience as Time, underlying the process of change, can be said to "shorten."

Interpenetration is the basic fact at the fourth-dimensional level of existence in galactic Space. At this level time is a much less rigidly definable factor than in the three-dimensional condition of physical existence and massive centrality. Interpenetrating fields of consciousness—old and young stars—can share their experience. One may assume that group evolution is more basic than individual evolution. The evolution of the whole conditions that of the parts. Community conditions individuality. But *conditioning* at that level cannot mean *control* by a centralized power. As we have seen, there is no really "centralized" power; no massive ruler or bureaucracy. The emergent power of fifth-dimensional space *does not remain at the center*. It operates everywhere. At the reflected level of physicality, it operates as the omnipresence of hydrogen.

An identical center of creativity is power within every star; yet every star performs its role in the harmony of the galactic whole, and there are an immense number of roles—at least it seems so to us as we watch the play of lights on the physical screen of our celestial sphere.

In two-dimensional symbolization, this sphere is a circle whose radius may seem determined by the intensity of the creative drive in the fifth-dimensional "Act of creation." But if this intensity varies, and we see this variation reflected in the difference in size and shape of the galaxies, it is because the cosmogenic release of energy-substance—as far as we can understand it through its effects—operates in a dualistic manner. Whatever is originally released always works its way outward in two directions. At the mechanicophysical level we speak of clockwise and counterclockwise motion or spin; at the more qualitative metapsychological level, we can state that once a new *potentiality of existence* becomes actualized, the process of actualization is bound to lead both to "success" and to "failure."

Bipolarity is the law of existence, at least as far as we can imagine existence in concrete fact. Existence is a cyclic process, and at the end of any cyclic manifestation we find both success and failure, or in the symbolism of annual vegetation, both seed and decaying leaves. Every cycle of existence leaves some *unfinished business,* some leftover or waste products. A new cycle has therefore to be initiated—a new cosmogenic release of energy has to radiate centrifugally from the fifth into the fourth dimension of space—so that the remains of the past cycle (its "karma") may be dealt with. The chemicals constituting the humus produced by the decomposition of once living substances have to be given a "second chance" to participate in the wholeness of organic existence.

If absolute—yet dynamic—Harmony is the supreme foundation of all existence at all levels, the dualism of success and failure at the close of a cosmic cycle cannot possibly last—that is, it cannot last at the level at which time operates. Time operates wherever one can think of existence, in the real sense of the term (*ex*-istence). Without time there can be no process, no sequence of states or phases in a cyclic type of activity, no activity, no motion. The manner in which men have felt the power of time and measured the serial character of existential events is susceptible of many variations, because human consciousness can *experience and interpret change* in many ways. But this fact does not affect the fundamental inevitability of time. If the supreme condition of existence can be symbolized by the Great Breath of Brahma, this symbol also implies change, process, and time. The only state that would be "beyond" this would be that of a consciousness able to dwell perpetually and changelessly in the realization of the unchanging *equilibrium* of these two perfectly compensatory phases. It is to such a state of consciousness that Tao refers.

As there are cycles within cycles, it is logical to postulate the possibility that a supreme all-inclusive Tao—if we wish to conceive a summit to the hierarchy of cosmic wholes—can be reflected in an ever-diminishing degree of intensity or inclusiveness as ever lower levels of existence are reached—each level placing its own limitations upon the realization of cosmic Harmony. To this Tao-consciousness at planetary and cosmic levels I have given the name of "eonic-consciousness." Such a consciousness apprehends a whole cycle (eon) in its totality from alpha to omega states. It must be able to experience every phase of the cyclic process in both the direction of success and that of failure. In this sense such a consciousness would be immanent as well as transcendent. It would be a "divine" consciousness.[1]

God is the All-encompassing Eon—and interestingly enough the word "eon" is an anagram of "one." The concept of Eon is dynamic; it encompasses all changes within any cycle. The concept of *One* is static inasmuch as it implies, in the purest metaphysical sense, "one without a second" (in Hindu metaphysics *Advaita,* nondual).

The only way an individual center of consciousness could experience in some manner the power of that "One" is by becoming Its (or His) agent in our physical-mental world. This is the way of the avatars, who bring down the fifth-dimensional consciousness of a divine "One" to the third-dimensional level of planetary and human activity. God *acts through* the avatar—to the extent that the avatar is open, ready, and able to be the Earth-terminal of this descent of creativity and radically transforming power.

In contrast—though the two ways are related at every step— the mystical path leads to the realization of "unity." It may

---

[1] Beings developing along the path of disintegration, because they fail to relate to the purpose inherent in the creative act, are reaching toward unconsciousness and annihilation. In order to survive they have to feed on weaker lives and minds; but eventually are pulled into whirlpools of darkness.

nevertheless be a very high or low level realization, depending on the scope and inclusiveness of the attainment of a conscious state of "wholeness." A true realization of wholeness implies a more or less vivid feeling-intuition of the interpenetration of the parts of the whole. This eventually leads to a constant *experience of wholeness* and a *consciousness of unity*. This is fourth-dimensional consciousness.

A reflection of such a consciousness should illumine the mind of the astrologer as he seeks to interpret the birth chart of an individual person at a more-than-physical level. Events are three-dimensional experiences. The Sun-center in the individual may be able to deal forcefully with these events and control them; but unless it realizes that it is also a star it can only operate as an ego bound by physical consciousness. If the individualized Sun in the human being does realize that it is essentially a star, it gradually learns to find its place in the cosmic company of galactic stars, whose physical earthly reflection—alas, so often darkened by clouds or lured by mirages—is humanity. (1974–75)

101, 104, 120, 141, 146, 159, 196
Raaum, Carroll, 60
Reconstruction, 126
Reformation, 122
Reich, Wilhelm, 75
relatedness, principle of, 205
Renaissance, 10, 91, 97, 120, 122, 145
Robson, Vivian E., 189, 192, 199-200, 202
Roentgen, Wilhelm Konrad, 4
Roman Empire, 13,
Romantic Age, 98, 106
Roosevelt, Franklin D., 107; birth-chart of, 135, 136; and New Deal, 101, 112
Roosevelt, Theodore, 108, 111, 125, 126
Rosicrucianism, 36n, 187
Rousseau, Jean-Jacques, 92, 95
Rudhyar, Dane, birth-chart of, 130
Russian Revolution, 77n 89
Russo-Japanese War, 111, 124, 126

Sabian symbols, 61, 183;; Einstein's birth-chart and, 184-185; Eisenhower's birth-chart and, 184; Mussolini's birth-chart and, 185; Neptune, Pluto, Uranus and, 133; in Nixon's chart, 131; Pluto and, 88; in Rudhyar's chart, 130; Steiner's chart and, 184; United States' chart and, 134
St. Exupery, Antoine de, 75
Sankaracharya, 58
Saturn, as planetary function, 22, 25, 26, 29, 32, 33, 35, 36, 42, 43, 45, 46, 47, 59, 61, 65-66, 67, 76, 77, 85, 114, 128, 132; Jupiter and, 27, 44, 46, 51, 116, 170, 187; Jupiter, Mars and, 34, 40; Mars, Venus and, 46; Mercury and, 28; Moon and, 29; Neptune and, 57, 60, 107; Pluto and, 64, 65, 201, 202; Sun and, 27, 28, 35, 40, 77, 187; Uranus and, 40-41, 67, 76, 110, 187; examples of as planetary function, 105, 108, 110, 111, 118, 123, 126, 133, 134, 136, 187
Saturn (Greek god), 61, 87
Schoenberg, Arnold, 77n
Schrödinger, Erwin, 152
science, growth of, 5, 14-15, 158; modern, 5, 6, 8, 10, 14-15, 98, 154, 163
seed, 66, 73, 207, seed-culmination, 98; seed group, 168; seed ideas, 154; seed-period, 123; God-seed, 119
self, individual, 48, 49, 86, 101
Self, universal, 20, 48, 49, 68, 168
sex, 75-76; as love, 59
shadow, 32, 46-47, 71, 72
Siva, 50
Smuts, Jan, 9, 19
Socrates, 119
solar system, archaic vs, classical view of, 142-146; galactic approach to, 17-25; geocentric vs. heliocentric view, 3-4, 13; heliocentric view, 7, 13-14, 16, 20, 23-24, 101, 147, 165

soul, dark night of the, 65; mind, spirit and, 162
South African War, 124
space, 11, 27, 161, 178, 190; biospheric, 22, 23; fifth-dimensional, 204-207; galactic (transphysical), 5, 22, 23, 24, 25, 35-36, 40, 54, 70, 151-152, 155-156, 158-159, 164, 165, 190, 204-207; heliocosmic, 22, 23, 24, 30, 35, 165; hierarchy of, 22-23; time and, 8, 16, 35, 158, 205-206
Spanish-American War, 111
Spanish Civil War, 112
spirit, 137, 163, 164-165, 166, 167, 168, 169, 170, 173; descent of, 168; life, matter, mind and, 15; matter and, 50, 71; matter, mind and, 152-153; mind, soul and, 162
Stalin, Josef, 126
stars, 23, 191-193, 199-202, 204, 206
   See also fixed stars for individual listings
steady state theory, 160
Steiner, Rudolf, 59; birth-chart of, 183-184
Stravinsky, Igor, 77n
Stulman, Julius, 9
Sufis, 7, 122
Sun, as planetary function 182; Ascendant, Moon and, 128-129, 186n; as center of solar system, 3, 10, 13, 20, 21, 22, 25, 26, 27, 30, 31, 32, 35, 36, 40, 50, 54, 67, 74, 83, 84, 89, 94, 114, 116, 120, 143-144, 155, 165, 169, 177, 182, 185, 189, 192, 209; earth and, 83-84, 87-88, 182; Mercury, Venus and, 26, 34, 40; vs. Moon, as light of day, 14, 83, 143-144, 176, 187; Saturn and, 27, 28, 35, 40, 77, 187; as soul 180; as star, 20-21, 23, 25, 26, 28, 36, 48, 59, 67, 84, 147-149, 155, 165-166, 169, 181, 183, 190, 192, 193, 209; Uranus and, 40-41; examples of as planetary function, 106, 107, 110, 114, 127n, 135, 136, 178, 184, 189, 200, 201
Surrealism, 112
symbol, 49; Andromeda Galaxy as, 164; in astrology, 60n-61, 175; astronomy as, 175; Christ as, 164; galaxy as, 33; hydrogen as, 164; in language, 195; in mathematics, 6; necessity of, 6
"synchronicity", 13

Tao, 205, 208
Tarot, 61
technology, growth of, 90, 99, 101, 112, 134; implications of growth of, 15, 154; Industrial Revolution and, 96; Virgo and, 92
Thales of Miletus, 179
theosophy, 36n, 73; Theosophical Society, 98
time, fifth-dimensional, 205-207; galactic, 159; space and, 8, 16, 35, 158, 205-206
Titus, David, 30
Tombaugh, C.W., 88
totalitarianism, 47, 78
Toynbee, Arnold, 199

transcendence, 167, 183, fifth dimension of reality and, 205; galactic consciousness and, 85, 155, 156, 169, 171, 196; galactic space and, 54; hydrogen and, 153; Neptune and, 56; Pluto and, 69, 75; of Saturnian consciousness, 35, 47, 61; Tantric process and, 55; of time and space, 8; in transpersonal relationships, 168

transformation, 27, 60, 86, 90, 174; astrology and, 173, 179, 185, 194; fifth-dimensional consciousness and, 208; galactic consciousness and process of, 25, 37, 85, 117, 141, 159, 163, 181, 196; myths and, 87; Neptune and process of, 59, 61, 106; Neptune and Pluto and process of, 188; Part of Fortune, Part of Spirit and, 129; "Path" and process of, 36; periods of consciousness and, 141; Pluto and process of, 92; 98, 99; process of, 8, 9; Siva and, 50; suffering and process of, 67-68; Uranus, Neptune and Pluto and process of, 25, 33, 35, 36, 40, 44-45, 65, 67, 114, 132, 136-137, 169, 172, 185, 186, 188; Uranus and Pluto and process of, 187; Uranus and Saturn and process of, 187; Uranus and process of, 39, 41, 52, 54, 112 *See also Point of transformation, Path of Initiation and Transformation*

transmutation, 114; Neptune and, 39, 55; Pluto and, 65, 71; suffering and, 71; Uranus, Neptune and Pluto and, 43, 86

transpersonal approach to reality, 98, 167, 168, 181, 195

transsubstantiation, Pluto and, 39, 71; suffering and, 71; Sun and, 155-156

Triptych: The Illumined Road, 26n

unconscious, 47; Neptune and, 47, 101; Pluto and, 69, 71, 76, 97, 170

United Nations, 102

United States, 106; birth-chart of, 94, 95-96, 110, 111, 123-125, 127, 129-130, 133-136, 187, 200; Constitution, 96, 122; Declaration of Independence, 96, 101

universe, "commonsense" vs. "dematerialized" view of, 4-5, 10; as a projection of human need, 6-7

Urania, 61n

Uranus, as planetary function, 37, 42, 120, 170; Neptune and, 31, 32, 41, 44-62, 65, 72, 99-100, 125, 127, 129-131; Neptune, Pluto and, 22, 25, 26, 33, 35, 38, 39, 43, 45, 47, 48, 65, 67, 79, 87, 114, 115n, 127, 131-136, 169, 172, 182, 185, 186, 188-189; Neptune, Pluto, Proserpine and, 25, 67, 87; Pluto and, 123-125; Saturn and, 40-41, 67, 76, 110, 187; Sun and, 40-41; duration of orbit, 86, 116; examples of as planetary function, 92, 124, 127, 202; (Historical) in Aries, 112, 113, 117, 118, 123, 132, 133; in Taurus, 110, 112, 113, 114, 117, 134, 135; in Gemini, 109, 113, 114, 135; in Cancer,

113, 126; in Leo, 86, 113; in Virgo, 113-114, 123, 125, 135, 187; in Libra, 86, 93-94, 110, 127, 184; in Scorpio, 110; in Sagittarius, 110, 111; in Capricorn, 104, 105, 111, 126; in Aquarius, 106, 111-112, 133; in Pisces, 112

utopias, 56

Venus, as planetary function, Mars and, 28, 29, 44, 46, 187; Kumaras and, 46n; Mars, Mercury and, 116; Mars, Pluto and, 42; Mars, Saturn and, 46; Mercury and, 26, 61, 189; Mercury, Sun and, 26, 34, 40; examples of as planetary function, 105, 110, 123, 134, 135, 200, 201, 202

Victoria, 124

Victorian Age, 97, 106, 110

Vietnam War, 92, 108, 123, 187

Vitalistic Ages, 11

See also Archaic Period

Void, 79

Wagner, Richard, 77n

Wallace, Henry, 74

War of Independence (United States), 109

Watergate, 50, 62, 94, 126, 136

We Can Begin Again—Together, 19n, 168n

white holes, 5, 156, 162, 204, 205

White Lodge, 24, 47

Wilson, Woodrow, 100, 108, 133, 146

Woodruff, Sri, 153n

World Institute Council, 9

World War I, 89, 93, 98, 100, 104, 108, 111, 126, 134, 185

World War II, 90, 100, 101, 112, 127, 134, 159n

Yin and Yang, 12, 50, 151, 205, 206

yoga, 43, 113

zen, *See Buddhism*

Zimmer, Heinrich, 144n

zodiac, tropical, 67, 110; tropical vs. sidereal, 83-84, 176

Zoroaster, 118

March 23, 1895 – September 13, 1985

DANE RUDHYAR A Seed Man

Dane Rudhyar was born in Paris, France on March 23, 1895. Quite early in his life, Rudhyar intuitively came to realize two things which have deeply influenced his entire life and work: (1) Time is cyclic, and the Law of cycles describes all civilizations as well as all existence; (2) Western Civilization is now in what could be symbolically called the autumn phase of its period of existence. As these realizations developed into a personal commitment to the future which he envisioned, Rudhyar felt the urge to divorce himself from Europe and to seek a "New World" -a land into which he could, as it were, sow himself as a seed, carrying within his being the legacy of whatever was viable and constructive in the European past. In the late fall of 1916, he came to America, leaving behind his native land arid ancestral French culture as well as his family name, Chenneviere. The change of name was symbolic of a total dedication to his ideal: the transformation of our civilization, a 'revaluation of all values: He became known as Rudhyar; a name derived from the Sanskrit root Rudra implying dynamic action and the electrical power released during storms. The god Rudra in the Vedas is the Destroyer and Regenerator, the transforming energy, breaker of old molds and the power of will or vital force.

This sense of destiny released through Rudhyar tremendous energy which he has channeled into the development of his philosophical ideas; through Music and the use of tone; through Painting as the Art of Gestures; through Astrology as a symbolic language with the potential to bring individuals in tune with cosmic cycles. Throughout his long life and his use of many different forms of expression, his purpose has became ever more clearly focused and dynamic. He calls forth the need for individuals with holistic vision and a 'transpersonal' approach to life to serve as the foundation of a global society.

I am privileged to publish the books of Rudhyar, beloved mentor and friend, internationally acclaimed Astrologer, composer, poet, artist and philosopher, who initiated the concept of a cyclic and transpersonal approach to life. Rudhyar's pioneering work, seeded generations of astrologers globally, inspiring a wholistic approach to contemporary personal and global crisis.

Barbara Somerfield, Publisher 2004

AURORA ☀ PRESS

For a complete catalog
write, fax, or email:

Aurora Press
PO Box 573
Santa Fe, N.M. 87504

Fax 505 982-8321
www.Aurorapress.com
Email: Aurorep@aol.com

Credit Card Orders Only
Fax 734 995-8535
Tel. 888 894-8621
Outside USA 734 995-8541